D1485211

CLIFFS OF INSANITY

www.transworldbooks.co.uk
www.transworldireland.ie

CLIFFS OF INSANITY

A Winter on Ireland's Big Waves

Keith Duggan

TRANSWORLD IRELAND

TRANSWORLD IRELAND
an imprint of The Random House Group Limited
20 Vauxhall Bridge Road, London SW1V 2SA
www.transworldbooks.co.uk

First published in 2012 by Transworld Ireland,
a division of Transworld Publishers

A CIP catalogue record for this book
is available from the British Library.

ISBN 9781848271302

L213,726l

Addresses for Random House Group Ltd companies outside the UK
can be found at: www.randomhouse.co.uk
The Random House Group Ltd Reg. No. 954009

The Random House Group Limited supports the Forest Stewardship Council (FSC®), the
leading international forest-certification organization. Our books carrying the
FSC label are printed on FSC®-certified paper. FSC is the only forest-certification
scheme endorsed by the leading environmental organizations, including Greenpeace.
Our paper procurement policy can be found at www.randomhouse.co.uk/environment

Typeset in 12½/16pt Erhardt by
Kestrel Data, Exeter, Devon.
Printed and bound in Great Britain by
Clays Ltd, Bungay, Suffolk.

2 4 6 8 10 9 7 5 3 1

MIX
Paper from
responsible sources
FSC® C016897

To Siobhan, Rory and Ruby with love and thanks.

Contents

'To be yourself in a world that is constantly trying to make you something else is the greatest accomplishment.'

Ralph Waldo Emerson

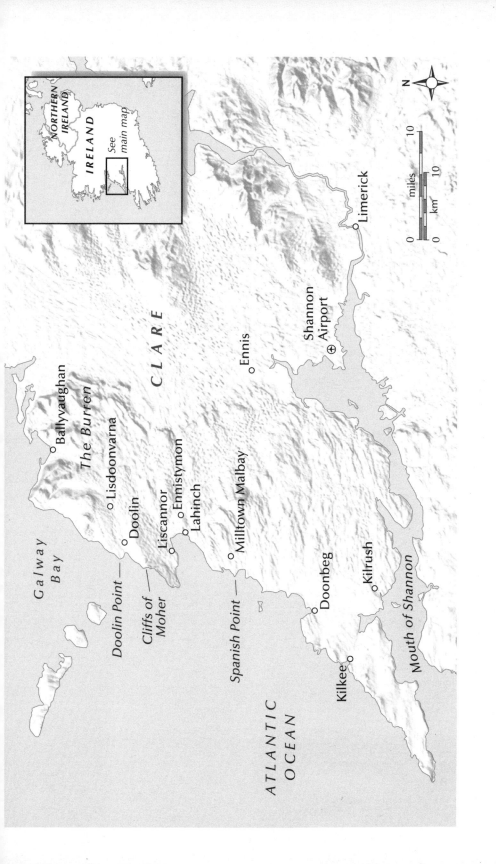

NORTHERN
IRELAND

IRELAND

See
main map

N

10

10

miles

km

Limerick

Shannon
Airport

CLARE

Ennis

Galway
Bay

Ballyvaughan

The Burren

Lisdoonvarna

Doolin

Doolin Point

Liscannor

Ennistymon

Lahinch

Cliffs of
Moher

Milltown Malbay

Spanish Point

Doonbeg

Kilrush

Mouth of Shannon

Kilkee

ATLANTIC
OCEAN

CLIFFS OF INSANITY

Introduction

You could hear the lambeg crash of the wave before you saw them, lost in it.

This was on a dazzling September afternoon at a patch of lunar coast in County Clare bashed by big emerald barrels of water.

You would never find the place without precise directions. It isn't a million miles from Doonbeg village but you have to make a sharp turn at such-and-such's unpainted bungalow and skip the first side road and look out for the school, and the narrow lane you eventually end up on promises to lead to nothing but a dead end. And in a way, it does: it brings you to land's end but the upward slope of the road obscures the sea until the very last second. When they are surfing there you will find vans and cars not so much parked as ditched in the unkempt hedgerows, and not until you climb over the barbed-wire fencing and stand on the grassy bank will the wave show itself. It is so loud and spectacular and breaks so shockingly close to the vast rocky platform that it seems like a bit of a joke that nobody knew about it for so long.

The wave and the place have become known as Riley's. It was discovered by surfers in the last five years and only then because of the persistence of a roving Cornishman named Mickey Smith. He was out there among them on this day, although from the cliff's edge it was difficult to make out who was who. From the headland you could see them in the water; black shadows on surfboards circling the wave.

'It won't be "big" big, just good fun,' Fergal Smith had promised on the phone the day before. The Mayo man is only twenty-four and has, over the last few years, opened a portal to big wave surfing in Ireland and been the chief subject of the ethereally beautiful photographs which Mickey Smith takes of people surfing waves. The best of these images have never been seen; others appear in surf publications, and every so often one might show up in an Irish newspaper or magazine, but always, always they catch the eye because of their jaw-dropping clarity and beauty. And perhaps also because the child in everyone instinctively wants to know what *that* must be like: to glide through the canopy of an ocean wave. It looks like what it is: a form of magic. Smith's photographs are so detailed that you can see the expression on the faces of Fergal Smith or Tom Lowe or Tom Gillespie during those few seconds when they are in the heart of the wave. Sometimes they appear to be in a trance.

They are all hooked on this. A bunch of them, Cornish and Irish lads, fell into a kind of loose confederacy based on their mutual love of surfing waves and, in particular, the pure-ice big waves sculpted by Irish winters. They all live sufficiently close to the key waves in Clare – Aileen's, Riley's, Bumbaloids – to enable them to move from their kitchen sinks to the Atlantic in less than half an hour. They study online weather charts the way novices read scriptures and given half a chance they can switch into meteorological geek mode. Any idea that you might have about surfing, formed maybe from the dreamy classics of the Beach Boys or the zanier moments in *Point Break* or floral-scented travel articles about Hawaii, can be torn up when it comes to this group.

To begin with, it is not as if they go to the cinema or the pub together or hang out in any conventional sense. They are only a group because they congregate around the same patch of ocean whenever the swell dictates and because they were all present around the time when Aileen's, the wave beneath the Cliffs of Moher, was first surfed, in the autumn of 2006.

Beyond the water, they have different lives. Tom Doidge-Harrison is both an engineer and a board-shaper. Dave Blount works in IT. Tom Lowe lives in Spain and his appearances in Clare coincide with anticipated ocean swells. John McCarthy runs a surf school in Lahinch. Tom Gillespie studies economics, Hugo Galloway science. Seamus McGoldrick swapped astrophysics for traditional music. The Skajarowski brothers, Dan and Steph, work in the tourist industry in the summer and surf all winter. Bill Keane is what he always has been: a sometime carpenter and sometime mystic. Mickey has his music and film making and photography.

But Fergal Smith is a surfer, pure and simple. He was in school in Mayo during the fast years in Ireland, when all voices were full of money and when the ambition common to all smart kids was to make a pile. Smith was profoundly uninterested in all of that. By the time he was fifteen he wanted to 'be' a surfer. As a career, it promised nothing more than penury and obscurity. To his peers, he might as well have said he wanted to be a priest. And maybe that would not have been so far off the mark because from the beginning surfing was more of a vocation than a pastime for him. A handful of talented Irish surfers have come and gone down the years but the idea of trying to make a living from surfing in Ireland was preposterous. It was what Australians or Hawaiians did, not Irishmen. Still, Smith went for it. He didn't permit himself the safety-net of a college course or a trade, he just dedicated himself to surfing. He has the ascetic self-discipline of any Olympic athlete. He trains on land and in the water and isn't bothered with night life. They all have tolerance for cold water but Smith sometimes lasts for eight hours on briny winter days, fighting ceaseless Atlantic currents and cutting nor'easterlies just to ride three or four waves that he is completely happy with. He eats frugally during these marathon sessions and seems to have a squirrel's constitution for storing energy. The glamour is an illusion: they all like to say that surfing must be the only sport in the world where you have no choice but to piss yourself several times a day.

Fergal Smith lost whatever interest he had in competitive surfing years ago. He likes it best when there is absolutely nobody around. Those are the moments when he surfs at his freest and when Mickey Smith ends up with photographs that keep. Fergal is the youngest of this group but he has flung himself into this idea of exploring how Irish waves can be surfed with such terrific energy and faith that he sometimes seems like an older brother to all of them.

If they share a common trait, it is politeness. They are quietly spoken and friendly lads and they are stealthy in their ways. No showboating or talking it up. They go about their days almost invisibly. Because of the weather patterns, they are often up at dawn and already in the water while the rest of the country begins to stir to the news headlines.

And that is probably the most important thing about these men and what they do. On those mornings, when most of the country is crawling along twilit motorways or coming off shift work and when the bulletins are echoing with grim and grimmer news and when you can't wrap your scarf tightly enough around your neck, there is a handful of people who are slipping into the Atlantic water to pursue something that falls somewhere between sport and art. And when they are doing that, nothing else in the world matters.

When you stand in front of the wave at Riley's or when you walk down the sheer trail at the Cliffs of Moher that brings you down to sea level, a strange thing happens. It is as if everything that happens above – everything in Clare and across the country – doesn't matter so much. The white noise and the worries of everyday life suddenly seem very distant. It is not as if these men are escapists. They have bills to pay and inevitable family dramas. Half of them have become parents over the last few years. It's just that they have learned to prioritize what is important. Most of them have been lucky enough to surf in the world's dreamier locations – Bali, Hawaii, Australia, Tahiti – but they have known plenty of weeks and months of living hand to mouth as well. They lived in Ireland through the years when mad excess turned molten, but they were too busy with the waves to notice or care all that much. And now that the riches have all turned to dust, nothing much has changed for them. They never lost sight of what mattered to them.

Occasionally, Bill Keane will drive over to Riley's and peer over the edge of the cliff at the mayhem. There were years when Keane had the waves around Clare for himself and he is thrilled by the revolution that has occurred over the past decade. 'That place is for the adrenalin junkies,' he smiles. 'Those bodyboarders are like a different breed. They are out for a different thrill. Bodyboarding was kind of frowned on when I started surfing. There was this attitude that anyone could do it. So wrong! The things that Mickey and Dan do out there are bonkers. Not many can do it. And Fergal . . . he is the only guy in the country who can paddle into a wave in Riley's. They can all get towed in but paddling is different. I am mad to go there and look at what is going on but I am usually off somewhere else when there are good waves. It is way beyond my capabilities, so good luck to them.'

If you want to see them up close at Riley's and have been told how to find the place, you have to be prepared to trek across a few fields that turn boggy in winter and walk through a herd of cattle that always look stunned with boredom. You have to jump a few watery ditches and climb a gate and then begin to walk across the long rocky ledge which is lethally slippery all year round but farcical in winter, when the surface freezes over. It is not the most inviting place to visit. Rock falls, from pebbles to boulders, happen regularly; the platform is strewn with smashed-up stone. About halfway across lie the dried-out hides of a horse and foal which fell from the headland a couple of years ago. The rock shelf has collapsed in the middle so you have to skip across a narrow ledge to get across to where the wave breaks. Most of them make that trek every time they come here, carrying their boards with them.

The wave at Riley's is glitteringly beautiful, and because it breaks so close to the reef it is exceptionally dangerous. Most of them have been scarred by it and still they trust that they will be all right there.

On this day, they were having a ball. It was the last Wednesday of September, 2011. In Dublin, the name of Senator David Norris had been added late to the list of nominations for the new president of Ireland. All seven candidates would promise to address the burning issues of the day: mass emigration, unemployment, despair – weighty words that had become as common as rainfall. The schizophrenic list of nominees – among them a former Eurovision winner, a Republican and a former aerobics instructor turned entrepreneur – accurately reflected the mixed-up, uneasy mood of the day. It was hard to escape the feeling that Ireland was a failed place. Except that down here, at this godforsaken spot, the mood was exuberant.

After Riley's was discovered, it took most of them a while to work up the courage to surf the wave because it is so confrontational in the way it breaks. But by this stage they had been reading it for years and were completely literate in its oddities. Sometimes they speak about it as if it is a living creature, with moods and quirks like any other. You just had to read the signs, be alive to what was happening.

They were in the water all afternoon.

The weather was gorgeous. Yet again September had

offered up an Indian summer and seven of them had the place to themselves. They whooped with delight at every wave made. For anyone there to hear their shouts the message would have been unmistakable: this is as good as it gets.

What they do defies easy definition. Fergal Smith's sole aim with surfing is to keep on exploring how far he can take paddling into big waves in Ireland and around the world. He always says that this is just the beginning, that he has everything to learn. The life he has chosen sounds and looks enviable from afar and up close; it often feels that way too. It is a life governed by nature.

But it is precarious. There is no 'career plan' and there is certainly no pension plan. There are periods, when the ocean surface is flat, when the days can be slow and frustrating. It is difficult to describe what he does as 'sport' because there is no prize and there is no beginning or ending. When you see him out there, he sometimes makes surfing appear like a kaleidoscopic presentation of the most extreme physical disciplines – ballet and gymnastics and boxing and anything that requires the difficult combination of exceptional balance and grace and physical strength. He just surfs, over and over, and accepts the bad days with the good. He leaves the house when it is dark, and it is getting dark again when he's getting out of the water. On big days he will meet up with Tom Lowe and Mickey Smith and they will spend the day surfing and filming and taking photographs. Sometimes he is on his own all day.

If this group has any message, it might be that the best of what this country has to offer is all about us – the water, the moving light, the freshness of the air, the wildness of the place. If they have an abiding belief, it is that you can't ever stop doing whatever it is that matters to you. What follows is an attempt to portray a year in the lives of these surfers in County Clare. There are other bands of like-minded people in different pockets of Ireland. But there is a general acknowledgement that the way Fergal Smith and Mickey Smith think about surfing, the way they try and surf in the wilder waves that visit the Irish coastline each winter, is something separate, and on its own. Together they form the energy which has bound together this accidental club who would never have met had it not been for a common love of those ever-rolling barrels of sea water. They have no idea how long it will last nor what the final outcome will be, which is part of the reason why they are living this life.

You have probably never heard of them, and they are hard enough to find at the best of times. But had you been standing on the headland at Riley's that September afternoon, with the country behind you in fretful mood and the sunshine lighting up an unlovely corner of Clare, and had you watched them surfing wave after wave and heard the whoops and yells of delight travel on the wind, then you would have seen them for what they were: in that moment, the most carefree people in Ireland.

1

Cloudbusting

A million footsteps had trampled over the fields of Little John's Farm and by nine o'clock on Sunday night England was darkening and the world felt drunk and happy. The crowd would sing out the end of summer. This was the last night of the August music festival in Reading. On the main stage Interpol glided through their set and a sea of bodies sang the chorus lines. Fergal Smith was somewhere among them. It was his birthday, and he had just returned from what most twenty-four-year-olds would consider a fantastical summer, spent hopping from Tahiti to Australia to Fiji to Indonesia and back with nothing but surfing on his mind. He ought to have been happy. In July he had achieved what he would remember as 'the longest, biggest, most perfect barrel I ever got'. This was at Cloudbreak, a fabled wave close to Tavarua Island, a tiny heart-shaped resort off Fiji. The swell had presented itself on weather charts a full week before the wave materialized, giving the best wave chargers time to book flights and rush from various corners of the earth to be there when it was surging, on 11 July 2011.

That morning had started with a punishing lesson for Smith, when he got caught on the wrong side of a gargantuan wave as the reef drained, leaving him standing in a faded T-shirt and shorts before a rearing mountain of water (think of a two-storey house) which sent him skating across the rock face, embedding dozens of coral fragments in his back. For the rest of the session he paddled with one arm because his injured side was too stiff and sore, but the next morning, out of the blue, he found himself cutting through this beautiful dream of a wave that had formed not only there on the balmy Indian Ocean but years earlier in his mind, when he spent school lunchtimes wandering the beach in north Mayo. That single wave made his summer; it was also a vindication of what he had decided to do with his life. He told himself that he didn't mind what happened after that. And now he was on his way back home to Clare and he was with Tess, his girlfriend, and they were standing among tens of thousands of blissed-out people, and he knew that this was a privileged life.

He ought to have been happy. But he couldn't help it: he felt wretched.

Just twelve hours earlier, Smith had flown from Tahiti into London. He wasn't long there when he checked the weather charts. There was no particular reason for this – it wasn't as if he was going to surf the Thames – apart from the fact that like all serious surfers he has a meteorologist's obsession with fronts and patterns. He needs to know what is going on out there, at all times. And what he saw made him feel queasy.

Even as his plane had left Tahiti, the makings of an unholy swell were beginning to bubble up, as if to taunt him. He had already amassed mind-boggling air miles over the previous three months, jumping from continent to continent on the promise of spectacular waves. He knew that nothing would beat his experience at Cloudbreak; not this summer. Yet he felt such a narcotic pull that he had to force himself not to buy another ticket and fly straight out of Heathrow again. He was terrified at the thought of missing a once-in-a-lifetime day on the ocean. And he knew that he was experiencing the perpetual dilemma that all surfers must battle: the junkie's chase for the true epiphany, the perfect hit. Logic told him that he was doing the right thing, but as he stood there at the concert he drove himself to distraction wondering what was happening on that small cubic stretch of ocean thousands of miles away.

The sheer torture of that evening stayed with him for the next few months. The forecasts had been right: the waves were spookily gigantic and intimidating, so much so that they became a trial of endurance and courage for even the most experienced practitioners in the world. On a damp Saturday in early October, Smith was sitting in his living room still trying to justify not being in Tahiti to himself. He lives in a cottage that is a ten-minute drive from Lahinch but which could take ten days to find without very precise directions. Outside it was raining softly and steadily; the sea was flat and the sky low. Smith was content just to sit, drink tea, and let the afternoon slide by.

'We were at this concert and it was great,' he says, recalling his mood that evening in Reading. 'Elbow, people like this, playing. But you know, you get one day like that and you don't know if or when it is going to come along again. I kind of avoided looking at the charts in the end because I was getting sick to the stomach. Ah, I don't know. In some ways, I'm glad I wasn't there. Who knows what would have happened? Nobody got hurt even though the waves were absolutely crazy and that was a miracle. So maybe I would have been the one who would have been hurt had I been there. Plus, I didn't really know anyone who would have given me a tow. I would have got a tow – I know I would – but if I was towed into a wave I didn't really want by someone I didn't really know – it's a whole scene and there is pressure and it is not comfortable. And you get smashed. And all for what? A photograph? Nobody who was out there enjoyed it, so far as I hear. It was just hell. It was up there with the scariest waves people have seen. Nathan Fletcher [Fergal's team rider with his sponsor, Analog] was there and he was saying that he didn't want to go but felt he had to. Nathan lost two good friends this year and he got smashed by two really horrible waves and he came out of it fine. So I think my not being there – the fact that I didn't see the swell – was a sign that I was meant to leave when I did. Now I feel kind of lucky because it was just silly and I might have been pressured into doing something that I didn't want to do.'

And then he fell silent, uncertain as to whether he had won himself over or not.

If Smith is certain about anything in life – and his opinion on most subjects tends to be definite – it is that it's not worth living unless you are doing what you want to do. He was fortunate in that he discovered at a young age that nothing would eclipse the feel of surfing, and since then he has shown a rigorous commitment to placing the pursuit of waves at the core of his life. If he had accepted his natural place on the surfing pyramid he would never have been out surfing Cloudbreak with a dozen of the most illustrious surfers on the planet as his audience. He was in the company of men for whom big pounding waves had been a natural habitat since childhood. Smith didn't even grow up on the coast.

His parents run an organic farm close to Westport in Mayo. He surfed for the first time when he was seven when his father bought a beat-up board for thirty Irish punt during a family holiday in Achill and handed it to Kevin, his older brother. That was it: the boys were hooked. But Fergal was fervent about surfing. He never thought of it as a sport or as a pastime. Rather, it was a way of living that he wanted to follow. For the next ten years he badgered his parents to bring him to the sea at every available moment. In the beginning he surfed with friends on summer days in Achill and they were every bit as good on a board as he was – the same knacky childhood balance, the same fearlessness, the same sense of fun. But he alone had this gnawing feeling every time he left the water, this vague constant longing that accompanied him through his day-to-day life. It didn't occur to him that surfing should be a seasonal activity. He just wanted to be in the water, all the time.

There are still folders at his family home in Mayo containing notepads that he began keeping in secondary school, their leaves crowded with ideas about what he needed to do to get better. He devised an improvised fitness programme, with push-ups and yoga and balance exercises. 'I was like my own drill sergeant,' he laughs. After school he began going to the gym and concentrating on sprinter's exercises – jumps, lunges, weight-bearing crouches – to develop his leg muscles. At school in Louisburgh he simply wasn't interested in the time-honoured ritual of traipsing down the town, having a cigarette and sniggering at the usual jokes. Instead he would jog down to the beach. 'Just to see the sea. I'd run along this back road and sit at the beach and make it back before the bell. I think the lads in the class thought I was completely mad but they were easy-going about it. It was a redneck school and they hated townies but I came from a farming background so I fitted in. It wasn't as if I was going around wearing flashy clothes and talking about it.'

When he was fourteen he felt competent enough to enter surf contests along the west coast. He got beaten, all the time, throughout that first year. Ollie O'Flaherty from Lahinch seemed to show up and win every contest Smith entered. 'I used to hate him for it. But the truth was I just wasn't very good. There was nothing for me in terms of becoming a surfer. It just came down to determination.'

The problem was that life kept getting in the way. It made absurd demands – insisting, for instance, that he attend school every day. Eight daylight hours locked indoors and no concession to the idea that there were waves out there: it seemed pointlessly restrictive.

He made up for it at weekends. The family had always been outdoorsy. For years, Fergal and Kevin had packed up soups and pastas and wet weather gear and a portable stove and had their parents leave them at the base of some mountain on a Friday evening and collect them again on Sunday afternoon.

They worked their way across most of the mountain ranges in the west of Ireland, camping out and learning how to survive in the damp haze of an Irish winter. Now they began using the survival gear for winter beach trips in Mayo, spending the day in forbidding waters and gales, drinking from flasks in between trying to surf icy, messy waves. 'We just grew up freezing and shivering. We got used to it. I was skinny as anything but I'd stay out in the water for five and six hours at a time. Then we often used to walk for an hour or so back down the road to save Dad or Mum having to drive the whole way to pick us up.'

It was, for the most part, a desperate, thankless pursuit, but it was all that he had and he loved it. He would come in on a Monday morning and listen to how his school friends had spent their weekend. GAA games. Nightclubs. Television. 'And I suppose I was asking myself: am I weird? I thought everyone thought the same way as I did. You know, you aspire to do what you want to do. When I look back at it, I was a complete loner. But it didn't bother me in the slightest. It wasn't that I was anti-social. I just didn't see the point. I wasn't in school for any reason except that I had to go.'

Then, at fifteen, he came up with a brainwave. Transition Year loomed and Smith discovered that by taking up a work placement in a local hotel he wouldn't really have to attend school. In no time he had signed up to become the most enthusiastic pan washer in Ireland. When he had acquired world-class expertise at 'pot-walloping' he signed up for life-guarding duties in the local swimming pool. It meant he had a legitimate excuse for not showing up in Louisburgh very often. So that school year was perfect. He showed up for his work shifts and spent the rest of the year hightailing around the country looking for waves. Kevin had a Citroën Saxo and they used to flatten the back seats and bundle their boards and whatever clothes came to hand into it and set off on tours to the handful of coastal towns that represented Ireland's surf spots. They were perennially broke but still managed to sneak in a trip to the Canaries, where they walked everywhere with their boards because they couldn't afford transport, and from there they caught a boat to Morocco and surfed the warmest waters of their lives.

When it came to returning to school for the Leaving Certificate, Smith was convinced that he didn't want to go. It wasn't the usual adolescent moan about education either, just an awareness that the system in which he was involved – learning sonnets and theorems by rote for set examinations and a possible place on a college course which would secure him a steady profession and a narrow, predictable life – held no interest for him. The very thought made him panicky. When he told his parents he wanted to leave, they told him that that was fine but warned him that he would have to start working. Kevin had graduated as a mechanical engineer and was leaving for Australia. It was agreed, as a compromise, that if Smith stayed in school he would inherit the Saxo, which would give him daily access to the sea. For the first time in his life, Fergal didn't have to depend on his parents or brother to transport him from home to beach.

He got his licence two weeks after his seventeenth birthday and slogged through his final year in school. His last examination in the Leaving Certificate was in construction engineering. He had started the day by surfing in north

Mayo and then showed up for the afternoon exam. The paper finished at four o'clock. He can still remember the delicious sense of impatience he felt as he was going through his final question. At home, his bags were packed and his boards were zipped up. As far as Smith was concerned, his new career began that evening. Except it wasn't a career so much as a vocation. He had his heart set on being a professional surfer whatever the consequences.

He made this choice in 2006, at the height of a decade in which Ireland had become slightly drunk on prosperity, a period when new wealth dripped from the nouveau mansions, the haute cuisine restaurants, the restored peasant cottages and the Land Cruisers and convertibles that roared along country roads in the summer. Smith belonged to the first generation of Irish Leaving Certificate students who were raised to assume that career and lifestyle ambitions weren't just attainable, they were a birthright. To the tens of thousands of Irish teenagers who sat their final exams that year his decision must have seemed as abstract and mysterious as entering the priesthood. Smith turned his back on the chief obsessions – money and getting ahead – and declined the safety-net of obtaining a third-level qualification. He just went for it.

So his mother collected him from outside the exam hall and he said good luck to his friends, who were busy making plans for the night's celebrations. Smith changed out of his school uniform in the back of the car as his mother drove into Westport – the last of countless trips with Fergal and his surfboard. He took the ten past five train from Westport to Dublin, got the bus to the airport and met up with

Hugo Galloway, a young Waterford surfer with whom he was friendly. They boarded a plane for Australia that night.

'I wrote my goals down. It wasn't a plan. More of a plan-slash-dream,' Smith says of that time. 'I wanted to spend two months in a surf centre in Australia, just improving. I was aiming to be a competitor then. I wanted to be the first Irish guy to crack the qualifying school.'

But Smith was caught between the luxury of having waves at his disposal every single day and a burning sense of duty to improve. He was still only seventeen but he was deathly serious about what he wanted to do. He knew that this wasn't just a fad, a lark for a few months before he rejoined the herd and signed up for a conventional life. He was hard-headed in his approach, and from the beginning, when he saw just how smooth and effortless his Australian peers looked in the water, having surfed every day from the age of six, he began to have misgivings. Smith was never under any illusions about his own ability. Whenever he talks about his early years surfing he never shies away from saying that he was just ordinary.

Others see it differently. Dave Blount, a Waterford surfer, felt as if Smith had just fallen to earth as a fully formed surfer when he first came across him. 'When you are in your mid-twenties and still trying to make the Irish team and this fifteen-year-old comes out of nowhere, you take notice. That's how it was. You'd ask: who is that lad? From Mayo. A goofy-footer [a surfer who plants his left foot at the rear of the board]. Has a brother Kevin. Any good? Yeah, they're handy. Then you go out and he has three off-the-lips done and you are thinking: what the fuck is going on here? It's true that there were a few guys on a par with him as a junior, when he was riding beach waves and normal waves. This guy Jamie Byrne from Tramore, and Cain Kilcullen would have been there with him. But then I had a session with him in Bundoran when he was about seventeen. I would have considered myself one of the better guys out there and therefore entitled to my share of the waves. But Fergal was sensational that day. He was on fire. Nothing relative to what he does now but I was just so impressed by his approach and the calculated nature of what he was doing. He knew exactly where to sit, didn't go on the close-outs, picked the right ones, got super deep, and he had this thing . . . the French have a word for it: *glisse*. You could see two surfers doing identical things but of one you would just say he has *la glisse*. Making it look a bit effortless but at high speed.'

Now, however, in Australia, Smith was confronted by the the near impossibility of his ambition. This wasn't the empty coast in Mayo or the Irish championships on desolate days in Waterford or Donegal. Suddenly it seemed like the world was teeming with naturally gifted surfers.

'Fergal was very serious about it,' says Galloway. 'For me it was more of a holiday than anything but he was on a mission to learn and the coaches there loved him for it. Fergal used to tell me when we were still at school that he wanted to be a professional surfer. And I used to think fair play to him, but I had no idea he would take it as far as he did. He was hard on himself during that trip because he felt he wasn't measuring up to some of the local surfers. But he was surfing with people like Chippa Wilson, who was probably the most promising young surfer in the world at that time.'

When Smith left Australia a few months later, chastened

and low in confidence, he chased the Pro Junior Peak tour. Along with Stephen Kilfeather from Sligo and a Newquay surfer named Mitch Corbett, he bought a van in England for £600. They followed the contests through Spain and France. They slept in the back of the van, ate cheaply and, as far as Smith was concerned, surfed miserably. He swore to himself that he wouldn't permit himself a single bottle of beer unless he surfed well in one competition. Night after night he sat stewing in the van while parties flared all along the beach. 'I didn't get to have a single drink. In the very last contest I made it through three or four rounds – which is still nothing. After that I was finished with the whole competition thing. It really hit home that unless I was living in that environment where you surfed every single day and were coached from a really young age, it was almost impossible to make an impression. So I came home really disheartened.'

But Smith inherited a strong work ethic. When he speaks, it is in the unmistakably polite and musical accent of west Mayo. His background, however, is more complicated. His father, Chris, comes from Cambridge in England. His mother, Bríd, grew up in Belfast. Chris was an engineer. They were living and working in Dublin. Kevin had only just been born when the realization began to seep in that they didn't particularly want the life of mornings stuck in traffic, of set timetables, of rows of identical houses and plumes of smoke rising from a thousand identical chimneys. It is the kind of nagging dissatisfaction that almost everyone experiences and is content enough to let pass. But the Smiths acted on it. They had been on honeymoon in Achill and were enthralled with the landscape and had a vague dream of one day moving there. So

Chris quit his job and they bought a house outside Westport for £14,000 with one acre of land and set up an organic farm. 'They knew nothing about growing vegetables. Dad had seeds and Mum had a book and that was it. But it was his dream to live a simpler life. I think that is the same thing as I did. Money wasn't behind it. It was just a change to a simpler, cleaner way of living. You know, Mum's from the North and Dad's from England but my parents put two fingers to all of that shit. They just did what they wanted to do. So I grew up aware of my Dad's work ethic: getting up at six in the morning and busting his back but never complaining and just being happy doing what he did. That made an impression on me.'

Still, after he returned home he wasn't sure how to progress. Then two significant things happened. In September he was invited to Indonesia by *Carve* magazine for a photographic trip featuring surfers from Ireland and the British Isles. He travelled with Cain Kilcullen, a prodigiously talented surfer from Sligo. The waves were just as had been promised – consistent, leering, immensely powerful – and the Irish pair won the competition that *Carve* held. Towards the end of the afternoon a particularly menacing set developed: big lazy slabs of water that looked murderous. The group was young and exhausted after the competition. Through a combination of impatience and curiosity, Smith paddled out alone, just to see how he would cope. He was a complete novice in surfing waves of this size and got by on courage and instinct. 'I was trying my hardest and kept getting hammered by wave after wave.' But even as he got pounded he began to realize that he had found his true fascination. He had always been ambivalent about the merits of competitive surfing: something about its restrictions and the happenstance arrival of waves had always struck him as ridiculous. While he had begun winning Irish contests at the age of fifteen, he'd never got much joy out of them. Now, he realized, the fewer people around, the happier he was. And he felt himself becoming fascinated by the thought of the challenge of wilder waves on different oceans.

He didn't think he had done anything other than get trashed about by the water but it turned out the photographer on assignment for *Carve* had gathered plenty of stills which were used in the next issue. It was the first time Smith made an impression outside his locality and he got a fleeting thrill out of seeing his attempts at big wave surfing laid out in the magazine. His mother was relieved as well. She thought that now that he had 'tried' big wave surfing, he would be content to let it be. 'She was worried. She hated it at first. I remember her saying to me: "You've done that now, that's the end of it." And I was trying to tell her it was just the beginning.'

The second significant event also happened that autumn, when Smith went surfing at Mullaghmore, the pretty seaside village on Donegal bay, around 8 or 9 November. Shortly after he paddled out another group of surfers arrived to go tow-surfing. A photographer was there with them, and after watching Smith paddling into enormous waves he jumped in the water and began taking photographs of this whippet he had never seen before. That was how Fergal Smith met Mickey Smith.

'I remember I just lobbed off the edge of the boat and began to swim over with my camera,' Mickey says. 'It was a fair distance over but I could see this big set pulsing through. Jack Johns got a wave and then Fergal. I could see them both kick off the back. Jack gets really excited when he sees something special – I mean really hysterical, like the girls you see in the old Beatles stuff. He was just going mad, and when I got to the line-up he was yelling at me: "Ferg has just got the craziest barrel I have ever seen." I was a minute too late to get the shot. Fergal was buzzing afterwards but he was quiet about it. But I had rarely come across anything like his whole approach to riding heavy waves. He was only sixteen or seventeen then, had no reputation to speak of, had no sponsors, and he was falling out of the lip at exactly the right place with all these freaky little ninja skills. It was just a vision.'

At that time Mickey was an occasional visitor to Ireland and had been staying with Tom Gillespie, a Dublin surfer he had bumped into one day. 'We all stayed with the Gillespies,' Mickey laughed. 'I think Tom's mum may have begun to tire of us. Well, maybe not of me but definitely of Dan [Skajarowski] and Jack.' His fascination with the west coast of Ireland was just beginning.

'What I remember is that Mickey was getting really frustrated by how the photography session was going and when he saw Fergal out there, he just hopped out into the channel,' Tom Gillespie says. 'And just before he arrived and got his camera set up, Fergal got an absolutely huge barrel. Mickey missed it entirely. He was very pissed off. But Fergal outshone everyone that day and I remember seeing the two of them on the beach chatting afterwards for a few minutes. And you could see that even then, something clicked.'

Fergal Smith had only known of his namesake through magazine work and through a clique of bodyboarders from Cornwall who regularly appeared in Clare. Mickey Smith had a reputation for ferocious curiosity and fearlessness and for taking sumptuous images which could make even the most treacherous of waves seem too divine to be harmful. Fergal doesn't recall much of their conversation on the pier at Mullaghmore that day, only that this slim, quietly spoken man in front of him seemed to understand instinctively what he was trying to get from the water every time he took his surfboard out. 'I only knew him by reputation: that he was this well-travelled . . . waterman, I suppose, and that his work was brilliant. I didn't even really get to speak much to him that day, to be honest. But a couple of weeks later he came down to my house in Mayo and we went surfing and got a few more really good shots in the waves. At that stage I felt privileged to be hanging around him.'

They quickly learned that they shared more than just a surname.

There was no formal agreement that they would work together; it was just that Mickey began appearing in Clare more often and seemed to have a diviner's gift for identifying new waves. And in what seemed like no time, Fergal became used to hearing Mickey's voice whenever he tried to push himself into waves that were just outside his threshold and range of comfort. Mickey had this way of making him trust that whatever he tried in the water would turn out all right. It wasn't as if he promised him that committing to the waves would be free of risk or that nothing could go wrong or that it couldn't end horribly. Instead he made him see that the risk was part of learning to understand what he could do in those waves. There was no braggadocio about Mickey Smith. He wasn't motivated by showing off or by making money or by making a name for himself with daredevil antics. He wasn't interested in anything, as far as Fergal could see, except pushing himself as far as possible to see how purely, how perfectly, the wilder waves the Atlantic produced could be surfed and then to capture those transcendent seconds on film. Sometimes he wouldn't even bother chasing waves himself, instead treading water with camera in hand, poised on the edge of a break, cajoling, encouraging and whooping with glee when Fergal or any of the others caught a good wave. He would stay out there long after his lips had begun to turn blue and his teeth to chatter; both Smiths discovered they shared a high tolerance for cold water. Mickey was brimming with energy and ideas and had the same attitude to the outdoors as Fergal, happily tramping the coastline for hours on wild days just on the off chance that he might spot another obscure break that they could attempt to tame and make their own. He could move from exuberance to introspection and back again quickly. 'Nobody else had his mentality,' Fergal Smith says. 'People wanted to surf these waves in theory but they were freaked out by it.'

The first time Fergal took his board to Bumbaloids, the wave near Spanish Point that Mickey Smith had spotted in 2005, other surfers warned him not to go out. He was standing on the rocks and Smith was out bodyboarding with some of the Cornish boys, and even through the surf Fergal could hear their kamikaze shrieks. Nobody had tried stand-up surfing at that point and he was at once drawn to the idea and terrified by the wave. 'Al Mennie [the noted big wave surfer from Portrush] was there and he said to me, "Whatever you do, don't hang out with Mickey." I suppose they were just trying to look out for me. People were literally begging me not to go into the water that day. Ollie O'Flaherty was there with Andrew Kilfeather [Stephen's brother]. We were looking at the break and they were saying, "You're mad, you'll kill yourself." And I figured I would just paddle out anyway. I wasn't going to kill myself by just paddling out.'

Fergal tried to ease himself into the break by paddling into a relatively small wave and was immediately taken aback by how sharply it curled and how close to the surface the reef was. Mickey Smith told him that he needed to surf the big sets; that way, the volume of water would cushion him. He was scared silly but he went on blind faith, and for the next three hours he arrowed through perfect opal-shaped barrels.

Hugo Galloway was on the rocks watching the session. 'That was the day,' he says now, 'when Fergal went off the charts.'

And that is what he kept doing, for the next five years. He paddled out and more days than not Mickey would be there, focused and alert and exhilarated by whatever challenges the water could present. They became work colleagues, after a fashion, and fast friends. For the last three years they have been living in Clare. Some Protestant streak in them relished the repetitive drudgery and hardship of surfing in a relentlessly inhospitable environment. It hardly seemed a coincidence that the waves Mickey had discovered in Clare were trouble just to reach, let alone surf. Riley's was tucked under the meanest rock shelf imaginable, an ice rink to walk on and littered with rock falls from above. Aileen's lay beneath the Cliffs of Moher and could be reached by either a choppy ride across the bay from Doolin or a daft walk down the sheerest goats' trail most people will ever encounter. Bumbaloids was comparatively easy but was notoriously volatile and would quickly accumulate a high casualty rate. The hardship involved in mastering these waves gave them every excuse to walk away. They took occasional summer trips to Western Australia or Tahiti, but for the next five winters the small stretch of Clare coastline became their canvas. There was no grand plan, they just kept surfing and taking photographs. Sometimes the images were used in surf magazines, sometimes not. Quite by accident, they embarked upon what must be the coldest and loneliest surfing project in the world. In the summer Fergal travelled to surf for his sponsor, Analog, while Mickey persevered with his photographs and short films and making videos for music artists. Clare became too crowded and the sea too tame in summer anyway. It was the tourists' time. They reclaimed it each winter.

The surfing community is contradictory: its span covers the entire globe but in gossip and scale it's not much bigger than a village. Stuff gets heard and seen quickly. Word of waves of rare size and quality in Ireland and of the skinny mop-haired youngster surfing them travelled fast. So when Fergal Smith began appearing in more established big wave surf locations, he found that he was accepted. He retains a perfect balance between confidence and self-analysis, still seeing himself as a novice in terms of where he wants to be as a surfer but secure in his conviction that he has already earned the right to show up at the choice wave breaks around the world. And he has always been diligent and smart about his methodology for becoming accustomed to a new place.

His summer began and ended in Tahiti. He flew there with Tom Lowe, his regular surfing partner, and Mickey, who had a week to spare. They had five days of brilliant surfing at Teahupoo, a phenomenally powerful wave at the extreme southern end of Tahiti Iti. Pronounced 'cho-pu', the wave breaks about 500 metres off shore against a reef that abruptly changes the water depth from over 300 feet to a shallow bowl and so produces frighteningly powerful waves. Tentative explorations of the wave occurred throughout the 1980s and within a decade it had become one of the most celebrated surf spots in the world, attaining notoriety in 2000 when a local professional surfer named Briece Taerea was pitched down into the reef and broke his neck and back. Taerea died from his injuries two days later. In the same year the Hawaiian big wave pioneer Laird Hamilton was photographed there not so much surfing as running for his life with an azure wall of Pacific water towering above him. Hamilton looks like the quintessential surfing frontiersman, blond and rugged and powerful, but with all that water behind him he looked incredibly vulnerable. He successfully made the wave and reputedly wept with relief afterwards. That photograph was the equivalent of the moon-landing shot in the surfing world: because Hamilton had been towed into the wave and successfully surfed it, he changed the perception of what was possible. In the decade that followed he would go on pushing the possibilities of big wave surfing, but that moment in Teahupoo left an indelible impression on a generation of surfers.

The Clare boys had visited Tahiti before, and felt comfortable there. So they spent a week just enjoying clean, excellent waves. On their last day the breaks became smaller and less frequent. They were due to push on for Australia and Fergal, usually so measured, paddled into a wave he would normally have let alone. 'Basically I wasn't in the right spot and wasn't meant to be there. I got a bit carried away. You could kind of feel the waves fading and it felt like our last chance of getting any big waves there. I got cocky and I tried something I couldn't do.'

In the film you can see him attempting to stand on the surfboard for a split second and then instantly bailing as the wave rises and the board is pulled vertical, literally pulled from under his feet, and then he is falling twenty feet through the air while the lip of the wave curls around him. It all happens in a split second, like a Venus fly trap snapping closed on its prey. Smith disappears in an explosion of white water.

He was driven towards the reef, and rammed his knee into it. 'I couldn't move my leg for a good while. It is not the best feeling because you know you messed up. I wasn't worried about what was going to happen, just annoyed that I'd made the wrong decision. You don't really worry about things going wrong because you could fall and break something at Lahinch beach as easily as there. Teahupoo is a perfect coral reef. When you come down the face of the wave there, the wave break on the reef is probably about five feet deep. So it's quite shallow in terms of hitting against it. But you would be surprised how lucky you get there. Sometimes the water hits the reef before you and is coming back so it softens your impact. It almost feels like a trampoline, hitting against it. You can get away with murder.'

But not this time. He spent two weeks crocked, fretting over a chipped knee and worrying that his summer would be over before it had begun. Tom Lowe headed on to Indonesia. Mickey returned to Ireland. When Smith's knee felt strong enough again, he was in the water at half past five in the morning – the first man out. The wave was about 750 metres off shore: it felt quiet and lonely. He stayed out there a full ten hours, catching six waves over the course of his day, most of which was spent straddling his board, watching and talking to the other surfers who began to show up at a more civilized hour. 'There were about twelve other guys and I knew a fair number of them at this stage. But you are always kind of concentrating too. If the swell is heavy and there is a set going and you are up there in line, it can be sort of stressful. Your adrenalin comes up and you are wondering: where am I, am I in the right spot, do I need to start paddling now, do I need to be in deeper? And then you might decide you are not going and you come back down and let the wave go. Everything has to be right – the wave size and the direction, and even then it could be someone else's wave. So when it is heavy, that's what it is like, all day. You are not even surfing, just reading every situation, and it is very draining mentally. It is a relief just to get a wave.'

At about two in the afternoon a local surfer named Michel Bourez showed up, looking as fresh as if he had rolled out of bed an hour beforehand (he would tell Smith later that he had done just that). By then, Smith was knackered. Bourez had timed it perfectly: a wind that was forecast for the morning began to stir just after his arrival and the sea glassed off for a brief period before the waves grew bigger and bigger. 'By this stage I was barely with it physically and mentally. I was making bad decisions and letting waves go by me. I was too tired then anyway so I just watched him getting wave after wave and it was brilliant to see. If you can time it like he did that day, it feels perfect. And Teahupoo, when it is like that, is probably the most powerful and perfect heavy wave on the planet.'

Smith spent a fortnight in Hawaii before flying on to Australia. For the past three years he has kept an ancient Land Cruiser there for convenience, tearing up and down the coast in the summer and parking it up for the winter. Tess, his girlfriend, flew down from Ireland to be with him and they met up with his brother Kevin and started roaming across north-west Australia. Just twelve days after they arrived, weather charts were lighting up with a spectacular swell pinpointed for Fiji. Smith wasn't sure his budget would stretch to another unscheduled trip but the trio began gravitating towards the airport while they worked out the financial implications. Their jeep chose that moment not so much to break down as quit, with no prior warning but with absolute finality. Two days and $700 later they were given confirmation that it was, as a sympathetic Australian mechanic told them, 'dead'. And then Adam Warren from Analog got in touch with Smith stressing that they wanted him in Fiji and that they would cover all costs. So began what he would call 'the best travel week of my life – a paradise week'.

Tavarua Island attracts water lovers whose wallets run deep. The resort hosts just thirty-six people at any one time in the tasteful bures shaded by the pandanus trees that run along the beach front. Mahogany furnishing and coral sand; no television; telephones by request only – the loudest noise comes from the fans whirring overhead. Surfers are drawn by the seven unique breaks and the notion of combining hours on the water with a family holiday. Diving and yachting are alternative attractions. Cloudbreak and Restaurants are the prestige waves in the water, and for most of the year ordinary surfers of a reasonable calibre can paddle out and tick them off, much as run-of-the-mill golf enthusiasts can experience the thrill of playing Augusta golf course through the fifty-one weeks of the year when it is not at the epicentre of world sport.

Fergal Smith vaguely knew that Tavarua was a luxury island and had long been fascinated by Cloudbreak but he had no firm idea of what lay ahead of him. At the airport he saw his friend Paul Morgan carrying a 7ft 3in board. Smith boarded the flight to Fiji with the uneasy feeling that his own board wasn't long enough. 'It turned out I was right. I was a foot, if not two foot, undergunned.'

Cloudbreak is a long left-running barrel about a forty-five-minute boat ride from the mainland. By the time Smith arrived there a who's who of the Hawaiian and Australian surfing scene had already assembled. Mark Healy, Bruce Irons, Kelly Slater, Reef McIntosh, Alex Gray, Kohl Christensen and Dave Wassell were among the faces he noted on the first morning. As in any sport which attracts advertising revenue, there is a circus element to elite surfing. There was, as ever, a heavy photographer presence.

The forecasts had been vindicated by the consistency and quality of the waves: it was one of the biggest swells of the last decade. Smith was exhilarated. Because he is a goofy-footer the wave was ideally suited to him. He was keen to see if his board would handle the wave so on that first morning he took off on one of the first breaks he could. 'I knew I wasn't going to make the wave so I just went straight. I jumped off and I knew I was going to get hammered. It was fine. But the thing about the wave is that it breaks into a point along this big long finger-reef. And I fell at the very start of it. So it peels down for about 600 yards. I wanted to paddle out to where I had taken off from but I kept getting hit by waves. You can do a big circle right around the reef and avoid the wave but it takes too long. And then the entire reef just drained dry in front of me. The water level fell below my waist and I just stood there waiting for the next wave and it pounded me. There was nothing I could do. It just carried me the whole way across the reef. My T-shirt got ripped off and I didn't even feel the coral for a while. I was just thinking: here I am in Fiji in front of the best wave I've ever seen and I have put myself out of action. It was game over.'

The rest of his day was about coping with intense pain. One of the boats ferrying surfers and photographers out to the wave was going back to the mainland and made a detour for him. Someone began picking coral shards out of his back and rubbed lime into the cuts and abrasions. His back looked as if it had been clawed by a panther. The sensible thing would have been to return to his hotel and get treatment, but there was no question of him leaving. 'This two-hour window of perfect twenty-foot waves. I felt like I had missed my oppor-tunity.'

The pain was hateful in salt water but it was completely eclipsed by Smith's feeling of having blown his chance. He paddled back out to where the main group of surfers were, his arm lame and swelling up, and stayed out on the water for a full six hours, stubbornness and aggression overruling the urge to call it a day. For most of that time he just kept his counsel, trying not to think about the burning sensation shooting through his right arm and feeling like the most privileged spectator on earth for this dream surfing scenario, as elite wave chargers like Ryan Hipwood and Nathan Fletcher got waves they would happily declare as ranking among the best experiences of their lives.

It was a folkloric day, the kind of rare accident of sea and weather conditions that this small band of surfers live for. Even someone who had never seen the sea before would instantly recognize that Cloudbreak is a force of beauty. The arc of the barrel and the speed of the water and the tropical colours make it look so hypnotic and seductive that you can easily forget its dangers. On the footage that began appearing on websites hours after that 11 July session, the place looks magical: sun-kissed and pacific. It is only when you see the surfers looking tiny against the enormous wall of water and the speed with which they disappear into it that the lunacy of what they are doing becomes appreciable.

For Fergal Smith, the rest of the day was a kind of exquisite torture. The journey from the beach in Louisburgh to this day in Fiji had taken five years but he was caught between two places, lost in complete admiration for the men around him and frustrated by his own injuries. He was by no means the only casualty. David Scard broke ribs after coming off his board. Mikey Brennan, a tough and optimistic Tasmanian, was so shaken after he disappeared into a churning wave that he decided to call it quits there and then.

'Mikey nearly drowned. He didn't surf afterwards. He got

nailed and came up and had a flotation vest on and he had it on over his arms. It wrapped up around his face so his hands were tangled around his face and he just couldn't get it off. And then an eighteen-foot wave just landed on his head. He didn't even know it was coming because he was struggling with the vest. He had no time to take in a breath. Ryan [Hipwood] picked him up on a [jet] ski when he resurfaced. There was no ski going out either – Ryan just took it upon himself to get this ski and go around picking people up before they started drowning. Another friend of ours, Dean Bowen, had a two-wave hold-down and if Ryan hadn't been there to pick him up he said he would have drowned. Without question.'

The weight of the water thundering overhead completely neutralized much of the experience of the surfers. Almost all found themselves in new territory and they got by on a combination of skill and bravery. The best were torn asunder in the water that day. Smith was watching Bruce Irons during the split second when he went from surfing the wave to being utterly at its mercy. The surfing vernacular for these moments is dramatic and universal: wiped out, hammered, chewed up, obliterated, etc. It is hardly an accident that these slang phrases convey comic-book drama because they are preferable to the more sobering reality, which is that for an unknowable number of seconds these men aren't surfers any more, just people caught in a place where they have no right to be – in the middle of a violently spinning cylinder of water which seems to have the energy of a living thing and which is completely indifferent to the fact that they desperately and burningly need air in their lungs. For those few seconds after they find themselves caught in these oceanic juggernauts, their reputations and all the other waves they have ever caught count for less than zero. As they lose connection with every aspect of the world beyond that wave, they become ordinary men – foolish men, maybe – in the lap of the gods.

But they have the wherewithal to stay calm, even when the water goes black and they are getting punched by their own knees and elbows and they lose all sense of direction, believing the ocean bed to be the surface. They wait and wait for the water to turn azure again, for some sign of sunlight, all the time holding their breath for longer than they knew they could. And most of the time there is a reprieve. But not always. There are occasions when the fates are simply unkind.

The shadow of Sion Milosky, a respected surfer who had drowned at Mavericks in northern California in March, was all about that group in Fiji. The Hawaiian had made the transition as surfing moved from being a relatively localized and underground pursuit towards becoming a major industry without losing any of his pure zeal for catching waves or his laid-back gentlemanly demeanour. Milosky had exhibited the form of his life on the very day he was pinned under water by two waves in a swell featuring twenty-three-foot waves and he was held under for that few seconds too long. He was a close friend of many of the surfers now trying to master equally dangerous waves. Nathan Fletcher, who had been at Mavericks on that March afternoon, had spent twenty frantic minutes scouring the water with a jet-ski before happening upon Milosky's body at Pillar Point Harbour Mouth. Milosky was thirty-five years old with a young family and was the first surfer to die at Mavericks since his compatriot Mark Foo perished in 1994. So his death was fresh in the minds of everyone.

'I had never met him but everyone out in the water had been good friends with him,' Smith says. 'Everyone in the water knew him. People were wearing these T-shirts saying "Live Like Sion". People were all quite touched by his passing. And something like that affects people in different ways. In terms of surfing, some people go one way – they are put off. And others . . . it seems to make them go crazy – just make the most of whatever time you have. But when you are out there, you aren't thinking about anything like that. You have a one-track mind. If the wave looks good and you are in the right spot, you will go. It doesn't matter how dangerous it is.'

Smith always insisted he was no cavalier risk-taker. He placed himself among the most inexperienced surfers at this break and he was one of two men without a flotation vest. 'You know where to get 'em?' he would flash back a few months later when questioned on the wisdom of this. 'I'd love to get one. I can't seem to find one anywhere. Only about forty surfers in the world even need them so they aren't exactly mass-produced.'

Back on that July afternoon in Fiji he watched the spectacular carnival of magical surfing and death-defying falls and he waited. He stayed out for a full six hours with his crocked arm and late in the afternoon he went again, committing himself to a decent-sized wave which for a few seconds barrelled around him, just to give him a taste. And then a wind came up and the wave became too choppy and broken and the group took boats back to their accommodation, battered and exhilarated. Smith passed the night in excruciating pain. He rubbed more lime juice into the wounds, took pain-killers, and applied some homeopathic ointment he had been given. He decided to resign himself to the fact that he was ill-equipped for the demands of the trip: his board was too small, he had no flotation vest, he had no knowledge of the wave, and he wasn't even sure if he would have the use of his right arm for paddling out the next day. He lay awake for most of the night thinking, and silently praying that the quality of the waves would be as good.

'It was a bit windy at first and the waves were all right. It was mellow out there. And then this set came. This guy James Sterling went first. Damian King, a bodyboarder, got the second wave. Then the third wave came in and it was way bigger. The two waves before had really cleaned up this wave – they took all the chop off the face. I was sitting beside Dave Scard. He had got one of the best paddle-waves ever at Cloudbreak the year before. He was shouting, "This is the one!" It wasn't huge, just big, and it had a good direction on it. So I decided I would give it a go. It just looked like a massive close-out but the reef is so perfect that the waves there don't close out. So I just went and pulled in and it was the longest, most perfect barrel I ever got. It was like a fairytale dream. I don't know why it came to me. I was just in the right spot.'

The film of that morning, which was posted on most surfing websites soon afterwards, shows Smith at the apex of the wave, wearing a light-blue top. He is framed in sunlight for a split second before the face of the wave extends and becomes a near vertical drop. He leans into it and allows his hand to trail down the face of the water for balance, as casually as someone leaning their hand over a rowboat so that their fingers can tickle the surface of a lake. His board and his hand leave parallel streaks of white in the grey wall of water. And Smith is crouching, like someone about to execute a dive off a board. Above him the lip of the wave is beginning to form into a luscious sneer, and with a barely perceptible transference of weight Smith adjusts his board. The water makes a perfect conical shape around him and suddenly he is in the middle of this beautiful barrel-shaped wave. This all happens in a matter of seconds, and he makes it look so easy and natural that it is as though the wave is doing everything it can to guide him and push him through. He looks solemn and relaxed, and for those first few seconds he was simply waiting for the liquid edifice to crumble about him and punch him into the sea. The white water seemed about to engulf his board but then this energy came from within and gave him another kick-start.

The film footage doesn't really capture the length and quality of the barrel. Some of the others told him afterwards that it was among the longest waves anyone had caught there. Dave Blount saw it online at work the next day. He had to get up from his desk, walk around outside, then sit down and view it again. Then he made a cup of tea, still reeling, and watched the film one more time. 'It was phenomenal,' he says, beaming at the memory. 'People don't realize. It was Phen-Om-Enal. People look at that and say, hey, Fergal caught a good wave out there. Look, Fergal caught one of the best goddamn waves that came through all day. You know this XXL big-wave com-petition thing? If there had been proper film of that wave, he would have been one [of them] there for ride of the year. No question. I thought it was unbelievable.'

It certainly felt to Smith as if he was in the wave for a long time. 'You don't hear very much, probably because you are so focused. So it is pretty silent and everything around you feels really . . . clean. I couldn't see the top of the wave at all because it was such a long high barrel so it was a pretty trippy feeling. When I came through, I knew that wave was always going to stand up for me. Guys came up to me afterwards and were hugging me and giving me high fives. People I barely know. It was a strange moment. And everyone else was jumping out of the boats figuring there was going to be waves like that for the rest of the day. I just felt as if I was crazy lucky to be there.'

Adam Warren flew in the next day from California. He had heard about Smith's ride even before he arrived. He had arranged for everyone to stay on Tavarua for the remainder of the week. After the winter in Clare, it was luxury for Tess. For a brief time Smith felt carefree about his surfing. Later in the day he was poised to commit himself to another promising wave but by the time he was ready Mark Healy had paddled into it and was gone. One second he was laughing and talking with Smith and then he was gone, over the cliffs. And it turned out to be probably the best wave Healy had ever surfed. Smith didn't mind. 'He was gung ho enough to be on it. Mark is so confident and so good that he made the call while I was still in that do-I-or-don't-I place. The queue system is vague when it comes to heavy waves. Everyone doubts themselves so if someone starts to go, fair enough. But all of that week was just fun. It was full-on luxury for us and it just felt good for me to know that I was capable of surfing those waves.'

Before the group disbanded, Smith went out to dinner with about fifteen other surfers. Nobody was drinking very much but spirits were high. Everyone was still giddy because of the waves they had just experienced and there was no bravado, no attempt to disguise the fact that they were impressed or excited by what they had seen. And these were the best big wave surfers in the world. 'They were all just buzzing,' Smith says. 'I had never seen that before.'

The next day, everyone split for different parts of the world. Fergal flew to Perth, from where Tess flew back to Ireland. Then he made his way to Bali to meet Tom Lowe, who had managed to secure him a late invitation to a contest there. Lowe ripped his arm in a fall and ended his day with sixteen stitches. Smith didn't even catch a wave. He then caught a plane back to Sydney, felt he should go to Namibia for a promised swell there, half wanted just to go back to Clare, but was duty bound to return to Tahiti for two reasons: his flight back to London had been booked from there, and he had, for the second year in succession, been invited to the CT trials for the world tour. It was another chance to showcase himself with some of the best emerging surfers in the world. But he was exhausted and he had jammed his knee in Indonesia, and once again his ambivalent feelings about surfing competitions rose up. Competing in these trials had been a distant, starry ambition when he was a teenager. Now it felt like something to be endured rather than enjoyed.

'There was a time when it was a big deal for me to do something like that. I think Tahiti was it for me though, when it comes to competitive stuff. It's a big honour to be asked to take part and I told the organizers afterwards that I didn't think I really deserved to be in there. You know, there are other surfers dying to get in and I just knew it wasn't for me. I don't think I should have to risk my life or push myself by doing that. I will go on bigger swells but on my own terms – when it is just you and the waves, and if Mickey is there to document it all properly. But to do it in a heat in an allotted thirty-five minutes with some guy you don't know is different. Big wave surfing and competitions don't work, in my opinion. It's great in some ways. There is money to be made there – Owen Wright won a pro event in New York last month and he got $330,000. But I don't think I should chase that because realistically I won't be winning any three hundred grand. I learned that when I was seventeen. There are so many really good surfers chasing that dream. And they might get ten places away from it, which is a fantastic achievement but doesn't really mean anything. The main reason I wanted to do the trials was a kind of Irish pride thing, just to have an Irish surfer in there and to maybe inspire some kid at home to be there some day. But it was in Tahiti that I worked out that every good wave I ever had, even in Ireland, happened when there was nobody about. In Fiji, there was nobody else on the water just then. I have never even caught waves when there are loads of people about. It just doesn't work. It is always half four in November and it is getting dark and there is not a soul around. Mickey will be over in the corner taking photographs, but that is it. That is how it is for me.'

And that thought was his consolation as he stood in that field in Reading. The glories of another Irish winter beckoned

– another season of shockingly cold and rough water, of twilight surfing and head colds and heavy beatings and the occasional head rush that comes with a perfect wave, and most of all the absolute serenity that will fall over him every so often when he is on the water at the time of day when shadows are already beginning to fall across Ireland and he knows there is nowhere on earth he would rather be.

2

Light Out for the Territory

For Kevin Naughton, the sight was unforgettable. This was the winter of 1969 and he was a fifteen-year-old Californian bored silly on a seemingly endless family drive from Galway to see friends in Derry. He loved Ireland, but the journey was a drag: hours of fields and dozing towns and not much happening. And then they came to a seaside town and Naughton idly looked at the brightly painted guesthouses and the pubs, a neat row of two-storey nineteenth-century buildings designed to obscure the water behind. His eyes fell on the window display of a shop called the American House as they drove across a small stone bridge. And suddenly there it was, stunningly close and unannounced: a perfectly formed six-foot wave breaking emptily in front of him. It was just a short paddle out from the shore and it was as if it was issuing an invitation, just to him.

Countless young men experience epiphanies in Bundoran

but most occur at about three o'clock in the morning when the nightclubs have switched off their lights. This was a grey afternoon. Naughton thinks he cried out in excitement – 'Stop the car! Stop the car!' – but his father kept on driving. In later years the wave would become known as the Peak in Bundoran. But that afternoon all Naughton cared about was that he had seen a wave that totally altered his perspective on this small, mysterious country in which his parents had grown up. That chance sighting was electrifying: he knew that lone wave was proof of others elsewhere, and that he wanted to surf them. He hadn't even considered lugging a board all the way across from California for this trip. But that didn't matter. He knew then he would be back, even though he presumed Ireland had never even seen surfing before.

Naughton was only half right about that. The first generation of surfers agree that the practice officially started in this country when Kevin Cavey assembled his best idea of a surfboard by fixing two buoyancy barrels to a wooden board and applying a pair of crude home-made fins. Cavey had read an article about surfing in *Reader's Digest* – probably Eugene Burdick's 'They Ride the Big Surf', which appeared in 1963. Cavey was transfixed by every aspect of the Californian surf culture and by the idea of introducing the sport to Ireland. The contraption that he made floated enough to catch the one-foot swells that moved gently in through Brittas Bay, and that was all the encouragement Cavey needed. He wrote letters to *Surfer* magazine containing photographs that were as unexpected as flares in the night: surfing and Ireland did not make sense; the place was just too remote and too damn cold. But Cavey persisted, and just three years after his improvised surf he received an invitation to represent his country at the World Surfing Championships in California. The organizers were intrigued by the idea of this eccentric Irishman wading into the freezing waters of the Atlantic: for many people on the west coast of America, the distinction between Ireland and Iceland would have been hazy at best. Cavey showed up and was in a field of competitors that included Mike Doyle, the glamorous Los Angeleno who was probably the best-known surfer in the world then. For Cavey it was important just to have Ireland included in the international fraternity.

It was around that time that he met Roger Steadman, who brought with him from Guernsey to Ireland the first proper fibreglass surfboard. The pair travelled across Ireland on a kind of a Lewis and Clark expedition. It was hardly an accident that many of the coastal towns they visited would later become beacons for Irish surfing. It helped that a handful of energetic people saw what they were doing and liked it. In Tramore, the O'Brien-Morans started surfing and never stopped. In Rossnowlagh, Mary Britton bought a pair of surfboards for her sons, and even though the boys weren't certain what to do with the gifts they began using them as rafts, paddling beyond the waves on Rossnowlagh beach and over to the nearby creek. It was only when they saw Steadman in the water in Rossnowlagh that they realized you were supposed to stand up on the board.

The naivety was part of the story: technique or knowledge did not come into it in those early days. Instead, Ireland's first gang of surfers were guided by the collective instinct that there was something about surfing worth pursuing.

They had the Atlantic to themselves for those early years

but it didn't take long for others to follow suit. By the late 1960s there was a sprinkling of surf clubs in Ireland. The sport would remain underground for the best part of two decades, but because the community was so small and because the practice fell somewhere between radical and deluded, it created wonderful solidarity and friendships between them all.

The Irish Surfing Association soon made its voice known, and by the late 1970s it had become sufficiently well established to send national teams to the European Championships, which were, in those years, frequently held in Biarritz. They discovered that the cheapest way of getting there was to sign up for one of the pilgrimages to Lourdes. The Irish surf team were treated like celebrities among the devout and the ill seated together at the front of the plane but were nonetheless invited to take part in the prayer ceremonies that began as soon as the plane was in the sky. They paid their dues at the shrine but never finished first. 'There would be four whole rosaries said by the time we'd get to Lourdes,' Brian Britton has said of those early trips. 'I remember once sitting between Rocci Allen and Grant Robinson, Ulster boys who "kick with the other foot" in terms of religion, during a recitation of the rosary. And they were there muttering, "Jesus, good job me auld fella can't see me now."'

This was the thing: when the bombs were going off across Northern Ireland and south Donegal had become a summer refuge for Ulster people, surfing was an escape from tribalism. The very characteristics that preoccupied the island for decades – nationality and religion – didn't matter at all out on the water.

The walls of the Surfers Bar in Rossnowlagh serve as an informal museum to the chronology of Irish surfing, bearing a montage of photographs sequencing the national championships that took place through the decades. You can often see tourists wandering over to look at one or two of them only to find themselves lost in the story half an hour later. The reason those photographs matter is that they capture just how tenuous the idea of surfing really was in the 1970s: it was still the preserve of the relatively small band of like-minded people who established the tradition. Beatnik beards and 2CV cars were the order of the day, and usually someone is holding up a modest cup or trophy at the end of a competition. But it's obvious that it is the mere fact of surfing that they are celebrating more than any competitive streak.

When Kevin Naughton returned to Ireland nearly a decade after his 1969 visit he discovered that a few local boys had had the same idea as him. He became fast friends with that first generation of Irish surfers. In one of those quirks of life, it turned out that his mother had been to boarding school in Salthill with Mrs Britton. Naughton's relationship with surfing seems both accidental and inevitable. His parents ended up leaving Ireland at an age when most people are just settling down for their fireside years. When he quizzed them on why they left, they told him that in the late 1950s it felt as if the country was in stasis. Nothing happened. Like most Irish people, they gravitated towards the US's east coast. They only moved to California after their son was diagnosed with a hearing ailment. A specialist advised that a warmer climate might improve the condition so they jumped to the other end of the continent, to Huntington Beach in California, the coastal town just down the road from Los Angeles which was and remains the epicentre of surf culture.

'My parents were Irish all the way in that they had the traditional fear of the ocean,' Naughton says now. 'I suppose they inherited centuries of a traditional fear and respect for the sea. I remember my mum telling me that the reason fishermen wore Aran sweaters was that if the boat went down, it would mean they would go down faster. There was a certain fatalism about the ocean that has changed so dramatically. So when we moved to California, they were happy for me to go surfing but they never remotely understood it.'

There was a peculiar symmetry about Naughton ending up in this part of California. It was, after all, in the waters at Huntington that George Freeth, the son of an Irish sailor and a half-Polynesian mother, gave his famous exhibitions in 1909 to mark the opening of Henry Huntington's spectacular Redondo Plunge, a showcase generally believed to have established surfing as a concept on the American mainland. He colonized the waters of Ventura, Palos Verdes and San Diego as surf spots and gave demonstrations of how to shape boards from wooden planks.

Freeth is a central figure in the mythology of modern surfing. He was already something of a virtuoso in his native Honolulu because of his radical interpretation of surfing – he rode the board standing up – and was also one of the first to harness the wave at an angle rather than simply milking the surf as it rumbled towards the shore. When he gave a few lessons to the novelist Jack London in the summer of 1907, London, delighted with the bravura spectacle of surfing and with Freeth's reticent, enigmatic character, rattled off a

swift article he entitled 'A Royal Sport', which appeared in
A Woman's Home Companion. It had the instantaneous effect
of bringing tourists to Hawaii eager to try out this exotic
pursuit for themselves, and within a few years the waves
crashing along the beaches of the US's Pacific coast were
deemed ripe for similar use.

Freeth became a folk hero on the Californian coast through
those surf demonstrations and his eye-catching grace as a
diver, but most of all for his fearlessness in his primary job as
a lifeguard. In one of his most valorous chapters, he ploughed
through storm waters at Venice Beach to rescue at least six
Japanese fishermen whose skiff looked certain to perish in the
waves. Freeth, as described by the *Los Angeles Times*, calmly
boarded the vessel and, seizing the rudder, managed to surf
the skiff and the terrified fisherman through the frightening
breakers and on to the beach, where 'girls crowded round him
just to pat his tanned shoulders and smile at him'.

None of Freeth's outrageous adventures on the water ever
threatened his life. He was actually felled by a more mundane
danger: he caught the Spanish influenza that raged across the
world at the end of World War One and was found dead in a
San Diego hotel room in 1919. He was just thirty-five.

By the time Kevin Naughton began paddling into the water
almost half a century later the fabulous exploits of this second-
generation Irishman were largely forgotten. But the sport
Freeth had helped to popularize had ballooned into a noisy and
irrepressible youth movement. In the 1960s, American surfing
seemed to be the subject of a constant tug-of-war between
the countercultural movement and commercial fashion. Both
wanted to claim it, for the fundamental reasons of soul and

money. Huntington Beach pulsed with the music, fashion and machismo of the sport. Naughton felt blessed to grow up in the midst of this vibrancy and learned to surf in consistently excellent waves. But he had to fight for them. Space was at a premium and etiquette took second place to bragging rights.

Maybe even by that day in Bundoran Naughton had begun to hanker after places where he could surf in solitude. As soon as he left school he moved north to Oregon, and soon after that he headed to Freeth's old stomping ground in Hawaii. But they were nothing like remote enough. He was just seventeen when he set off on a series of picaresque trips along the coastlines of Central America and Africa with a budding photographer named Craig Peterson, who by sixteen was already providing *Surfer* magazine with most of its images. They didn't know it then but they were setting the template for international surf trekking. They went with not much more than a few surfboards stacked into the original Volkswagen camper van and a fistful of dollars and sent back dispatches of their rambles and wave discoveries – a now celebrated collection of essays and photographs which received clamorous attention when they appeared in *Surfer*.

In retrospect, what they did was wonderfully reckless. Peterson was so young that he had to get a note from his parents to hand in with his passport before he was permitted to leave the country. 'Our folks were a bit innocent about what it was all about,' Naughton laughs. 'The early days in Mexico and El Salvador were perfect [though]. The whole place has taken a turn for the worse – a lot of crime and drugs. But then it was genuinely these sleepy towns with old Latin charm to them. The people were friendly. There weren't a lot of cars. And they made us feel welcome. There are a lot of cultural similarities between the Latinos and the Irish – friendly, Catholic matriarchal societies with a love of music. So people were very good to us. And we never had any fear that something bad was going to happen. Now, if you go down there you are a bit on edge. Is someone going to rob me? Is someone going to kidnap me? Then, you just didn't think like that because chances were it wasn't going to happen.'

They surfed in Senegal, Liberia, Morocco, France, Spain, Mexico and Barbados, and generally wandered so far off the beaten track that there was no track. In West Africa they found that the roads would end before they reached the coast and they paddled down lazy chocolate-brown rivers on their surfboards to reach the sea. Once, they passed through a village and the locals began to run alongside them shouting, 'Bill Harzy, Bill Harzy!' Naughton and Peterson were intrigued by the idea of this mysterious Bill Harzy, thinking him some sort of Kurtz-like figure who had been there before them. It was only afterwards that they learned about bilharzia, a severe illness caused by the parasitic worms that bred in local waters. It was one of countless close calls. Optimism and an unflagging sense of adventure sustained them. They lived on a shoestring budget and experienced the kind of getting-away-from-it-all holiday bliss that is now marketed in the glossy pages of travel magazines. In California an entire generation of younger surfers eagerly awaited the next bulletin from the back of beyond. What Naughton and Peterson did must have contributed to the backpacking phenomenon which would become a global industry in later decades.

'That never occurred to us then,' Naughton says. 'We were

just doing something we wanted to do. The first articles we wrote, there was no interest. But when they ran this one from El Salvador they were stunned by the response. So they said: where did you want to go next? I mean we had more in common with nineteenth-century explorers sending back field notes to journals than the current way of doing things. We just stuck these articles in envelopes and put stamps on them.'

Once, a tube containing Peterson's photographs and an essay that Naughton had written using beer mats or old envelopes or whatever materials he could lay his hands on arrived in the office of *Surfer* magazine. When they opened it a huge African bee came flaming out, intent on revenge for weeks in captivity. Its journey was ended with the hefty thud of a city phone directory. But the articles brought more than just wrathful insects to the magazine. After the publication of a story on the Petacalco wave in Mexico, death threats were posted and phoned to the editor Paul Holmes by gringo surfers furious that their secluded paradise was being paraded before the world.

The pair just kept moving on, returning to California only to catch their breath and the troubled flavour of America in the 1970s and to plan their next jaunt. They continued to send their articles on to the magazine in blind faith with vague instructions to post payment to a credit union at some town or other they hoped eventually to reach. Sometimes there would be money there, other times not. They lived with Kerouac frugality: Dan Pelsinger, whom they befriended in France, recalled his first sighting of the pair in the affluent beach resort of Hossinger as 'two guys in overcoats sifting through the sand for money'.

The calendar had rolled around to 1978 when they eventually hit Ireland. All of Naughton's hopes were confirmed: surfing in Ireland was still a genuinely underground pursuit. If he made allowances for the damp climate and the bracing winds, the country gave him a glimpse of what surfing culture must have been like along the California coast in the early 1950s, when it was the idyllic and largely ignored lifestyle of people just seeking an alternative to the mainstream. There was a genuine fraternity in Ireland that appealed to Naughton, and there was always the chance of turning the corner from a briary laneway just in time to see a sparkling, never-surfed wave on another patch of the Atlantic. Who wouldn't be seduced by that possibility?

'Yeah, that is so true,' he says of that time. 'Hugh O'Brien Moran is a distant cousin of mine and we surfed some waves in Tramore when I went down to visit. But when I came here to live I used to get around on trains and buses, and I saw amazing potential here. The key thing was that the technology in wetsuits didn't improve until the mid-1970s. Then O'Neill came out with this wetsuit called the Animal Skin. It was the first really efficient cold-water wetsuit and that meant you could go out for three and four hours and still be warm. In the beginning I just wished people would turn up to surf with me. I was aware that this was a really special place: world-class waves and just a handful of guys around to ride them. It was about perfect.'

By the time they reached Fiji in 1983, it seemed like a natural bookend to their adventures. A friend named Dave Clarke was hoping to open up a surfing resort there and he invited them to Tavarua. 'It wasn't anything,' Naughton recalls. 'Just a Pacific island.' The surf on the beach front was flat for the first few days, but when they were scanning the water with binoculars someone noticed an open ocean break. They headed out in a boat to investigate and surfed the wave that became Cloudbreak. 'It was about ten feet and excellent. I would say it had been surfed by guys passing through on yachts so I can't honestly claim to be the first to surf it. But we did write an article on the place and it began to open up. People heard about it and made bookings and the wave became known.'

And that is the magical thing about surfing: despite the vastness of the oceans, the surf community has always been fairly localized. Twenty-eight years later Fergal Smith would show up at that very same spot for that red-letter day in July. If you could trace the global movement of the Irish surfing fraternity over the last forty years, the pattern would present a relatively small number of faces showing up at the same remote spots.

Naughton would become a regular face on the Irish surfing scene, moving to Dublin to study literature at Trinity before eventually settling back in California. Mickey Dora, the most cinematic of the nonconformist sixties surfers, introduced him to the girl who would become his wife when he was in France. He can laugh now when asked about how hard it was to settle back into the routine and comfort of westernized life after that roaming spree. 'If I could do it again, I would just do more of it. But yeah, you had to re-programme yourself every time. It felt like being an astronaut coming in from space.'

*

The world was a different place by the time that Mickey Smith was wave hunting, but the spirit in which Naughton and Peterson travelled remained the same.

The quixotic search for a new wave has always been a sacred part of surf culture, and looking for waves nobody knew about was something that had engaged Mickey since his childhood days in Cornwall. Scouting the coastline of wherever he happened to travel to felt as natural to him as locating the closest supermarket to someone else. He literally had no choice about his first visit to County Clare. He was walking to school one morning in Penzance when a car crammed with a few older lads he knew pulled up. They bundled him in, sped off and told him that they were going on a jaunt to Ireland and that he was coming along. He didn't protest very hard and rang his mum from a phone box at the ferry port. In the years afterwards he found himself back in Clare several times and had walked long stretches of the coast, but he still shakes his head when he thinks about the first time he saw the wave at the Cliffs of Moher.

In December 2005 he was showing three Australian body-boarders – Brenden Newton, Adam Benwell and Harry Dixon – the best waves in the country for a photographic assignment. The quartet was touring in a van and there were some others trailing in cars, including Jack Johns and Dan Skajarowski. One afternoon they planned to paddle into waves breaking off Doolin, but as they were getting ready to get into the water Smith kept looking over towards the cliffs, convinced that he could see the white tips of peaking waves in the distance. On a calm afternoon two days earlier they had been sitting at the cliffs and someone had remarked how magical it would be if there happened to be a world-class wave in the area. Smith and the others walked from Doolin along the Lahinch road which levels out with the cliffs. So for the very first time he crossed the field, which was muddy and pocked with hoof marks and fell in a natural slope towards the headland. He just wanted to satisfy himself that there was nothing there.

'And I just remember walking over that headland and this big hollow wave just boomed in front of us.'

For those few minutes Mickey Smith felt like Carter must have felt after he had busted into Tutankhamen's tomb. He and the others were looking down at surfing treasure and they knew it. Smith's mind immediately went into overdrive. 'How the fuck do we get down there? There were vertical cliffs everywhere we looked and from where we were standing you couldn't know the goats' trail was there. The only thing we could think of was to paddle all the way over from Doolin or to hire a boat at Liscannor.'

John McCarthy was the only Irish surfer Smith knew properly back then. He phoned McCarthy from the cliff top and started babbling about this wave, this fantastical wave that had been breaking secretly for thousands of years. And McCarthy, well used to Smith's enthusiasms, simply laughed. Smith had already found and christened the wave at Bumbaloids, a ferociously aggressive wave that didn't so much break as snap like a bear trap. It dared you to surf it.

'This another one of your bodyboarding waves, Mick?' McCarthy said. 'Some horrible nasty wave that nobody wants to surf?'

Mickey told him that he needed a boat. McCarthy assured him that nobody was going to give him a boat at three o'clock on a December afternoon. He tried to tell his friend that he was just getting over-excited.

They stood there looking down at the wave. Brenden Newton told him that it looked like one of the most perfect waves he had seen. On that afternoon, it seemed unreachable. But they were already half possessed by the idea and decided to paddle across the open sea from the pier at Doolin on their surfboards. Even allowing for their sea experience, it was foolhardy. By the time they made it over there the sea was too rough to even contemplate surfing and the light was fading anyway. The cliff had become an incomprehensibly vast face glowering down at them. They had to paddle back using a Zippo lighter as a guide. Smith was due to fly home two days later and he had no idea when he would be in Ireland again.

Months passed. Smith spent most of this time on assignment for *Surfer* magazine, living in Australia and spending considerable time in Hawaii and the Canaries. 'It was killing me, the thought of that wave there.'

By the summer of 2006 he was photographing some of the professional surf contests in France and then in Cornwall. It wasn't deliberate, but he was gradually moving back towards Ireland. He had visited many beautiful places that year but the Cliffs of Moher wouldn't leave his mind.

In late summer he received a phone call from John McCarthy. Now it was the Irishman's turn to rave down the phone. He had gone up for a look with Dave Blount and had seen the same majestic curve and beautiful detonation. From the grassy heights, it had looked heaven sent. 'We had been surfing Crab Island and just decided to have a look,' McCarthy recalls. 'And it was there, just like he said. We saw the thing in all its glory. It was unbelievable to think that this thing had been there from time immemorial.' McCarthy had a plan: he and Blount decided to buy a jet-ski. They wanted to surf it the way they were surfing the Jaws wave in Hawaii.

The Tramore boys were, at that stage, two of the best-known names in Irish surfing. As Blount puts it, they were a kind of double act – 'the Laurel and Hardy of Irish surfing'. They excelled at surfing as teenagers and showed up at competitions together, and because they both had strawberry colouring and were outgoing one was often mistaken for the other. By 2006 they had visited most of the surf locations in the world, and as Blount stood on the cliffs that afternoon, his mind wandered back to a winter he had spent in Hawaii. In January 1998 he'd had the good fortune to be on the island when one of those epochal swells, known afterwards as 'Biggest Wednesday', hit the North Shore.

As it happened, the Bundoran surfer Richard Fitzgerald was in Hawaii at the same time. Blount and Fitzgerald met up the old-fashioned way: by accident. Blount worked in IT but isn't certain if he even had an email account at that time. Instead, during a brief call home someone had told him that Fitzgerald was on the island and he tracked him down and together they watched this fantasy day unfold. The conditions were so dangerous that the beach was quickly closed and police and lifeguards were posted at Waimea to keep people out of the water. When one intrepid local named Jason Majors broke the cordon and hurled himself into the surf, he was spat back to shore and re-emerged exhausted and broken half an hour later, when he was promptly arrested for his troubles.

But just a mile away, a group of surfers led by the redoubtable

Ken Bradshaw had arrived at an obscure break named Outside Log Cabins. It was there that Dan Moore towed Bradshaw into what was then estimated to be the biggest wave ever surfed. For Blount, it was an exercise in beautiful madness. A few nights later he found himself in the company of Noah Johnson, who had been among the group at Log Cabins. It had been Johnson's first time to tow in and he was still ecstatic from the experience. 'He was frothing about the barrel he had got but I was wondering about survival. To come from Tramore and see that was quite a journey but I didn't think: hey, I want to get a ski and tow-in like these guys. I figured I never wanted to go near a wave like that. I figured your bog standard Sunset. Waimea was plenty challenging for me – and still is.'

But when he stood there on the Clare cliffs with McCarthy that day and watched the wave breaking below them, the jet-ski made sense. 'The swell was doing the things that Jaws does – coming in, a big lump of water, apexing around the reef, bending into it and churning along in big barrels and spitting. So I was thinking: OK, yeah. Let's get a ski.'

They eventually located a ski in Newtownards. They spent some time learning how to use it at Spanish Point but were still fairly amateurish when, in late September, Mickey Smith phoned McCarthy to say he was back in Doolin. They arranged to meet at the visitors' centre the following morning.

Mickey brought with him Robin Kent, an experienced English surfer. Jack Johns, Dan Skajarowski and Danny Wall came along too. Tom and Fintan Gillespie from Dublin were also there – they'd decided to accompany the others just to have a look and then spend the day surfing elsewhere – as well as Seamus McGoldrick from Sligo. Tom had a hand-held camcorder with him, and even as he adjusted the lens to get the wave in his sightline he felt his stomach tightening. 'I still have that footage somewhere,' Gillespie says of the moment they saw the wave. 'Everyone was excited, lots of shouting – "Holy fuck!", that sort of thing. I had never seen anything like it. Shambles [McGoldrick] wanted to get out there straight away but Fintan and I were apprehensive . . . We were a bit frightened of it, to be honest. Mickey was definitely going for it. He is pretty open-minded about that . . . I'm probably a bit more calculated. I don't know: there was just something about that wave that day. So we split.'

The most unlikely member of the party was Rusty Long, the Californian heavy-wave specialist. Always attracted to remote waves, Long had been mooching around the Hebrides in Scotland looking for surf and, noticing that the weather charts looked promising for Ireland, had promptly taken the ferry over to Larne, driven down to Clare and phoned Smith, whom he had bumped into a few times down the years. Mickey then told him of this wave they were going to try out the following morning.

Long had put the hours in at all the serious surf spots, including Teahupoo, Jaws and Mavericks. But there was something completely apart and humbling about stepping out on to the ledge and seeing that wave for the first time. They looked down at Hag's Head and at the sea birds circling and the wave rumbling towards them uncaringly and they hesitated. By then they had discovered the goats' trail and could at least make their way down to the wave by foot. For a little while they were unsure. The morning was blustery, and after they'd all trudged across the field they spent some time at the castle discussing it. Smith was privately disappointed: the wave looked nowhere near as flawless as it had done the first time he had seen it.

'From above, it was hard to judge the wave,' Dan Skajarowski says. 'So we walked down the cliff and went along from the bottom and we paddled out. It was so scary. It was really windy, not so good a day. To be honest, the wave was dodgy. I wouldn't be too impressed if I saw it now. But I hadn't seen anything like it before. No way was I missing it.'

It was a stroke of luck that Long happened to be there. He was the most accomplished surfer in the group, and once he gave his imprimatur they all felt better about what they were doing. 'It was a conversation we were having,' McCarthy says. 'Rusty was calling the shots, though. It felt like a very big deal to us all.' It was Long who pointed out that even if they didn't use the jet-ski, it would nonetheless be a good idea to have it there for safety.

The three bodyboarders hared down the goats' trail, eager to get in the water. Mickey decided he would spend the afternoon shooting film from the jet-ski. By the time they had launched the ski from Doolin – 'None of us had a clue what we were at so there were all kinds of calamities,' Smith says – the bodyboarding trio had already surfed the wave. It is generally agreed that Jack Johns officially caught the first wave at Aileen's. The others followed. When the four boys arrived on the jet-ski, they spent a few minutes in complete awe of the landscape. 'It is such a spinner being under those cliffs still,' Smith says. 'We were just figuring out where to sit and hooting at these big empty barrels and generally freaking out. Then Danny Wall went.'

In real life Wall was a carpenter in Devon, but they all knew him as someone who brought a gun-slinging attitude to bodyboarding. He liked to smoke a cigarette on the water and then paddle into waves that made most surfers shudder. 'That Cornish-sailor gene,' McCarthy calls it. 'They all have it. You know, is there no fear of life?'

They watched Wall attack the wave with typical gusto and it cooperated with him for three or four seconds before mauling him. Wall disappeared and then resurfaced for a split second before the white water rushed over him and carried him right in under the cliffs. He circled around the wave and gradually made his way back towards the jet-ski, at once chastened and delighted.

'Fucken 'ell, Smith,' he said reproachfully. 'Wot you got us into 'ere?'

They laughed. Then a few minutes later Rusty Long judged his moment and picked off the most perfect wave of the morning, taking an ideal line and gliding through as if to confirm that the place was indeed somewhere special. Later, Long would write about the experience in *Surfer* magazine.

John McCarthy went and came through what he described as a small wave unscathed, then Blount followed up by paddling into a bigger, meaner version. 'It was a giant,' McCarthy says. 'Mickey took this amazing photograph of Dave and then the wave just came over him. He was pushed twenty feet down. His leash broke and the board just disappeared. It vanished. We never saw it again.' The photograph that Smith took of the moment is hanging in Blount's living room – an azure wave still exploding. 'I'm somewhere underneath,' Blount sighed.

Mickey Smith didn't even try to surf that day. He was just

lost in the beauty of the place and kept taking photographs of everyone else. The others were so wrapped up in what they were doing that they hardly even noticed. 'That didn't surprise me though,' says McCarthy. 'There were several days when I met Mickey at Crab Island and the surf was perfect but he was primarily interested in being the cameraman. He was focusing on – who knows Mickey's mind, but yeah, on capturing this unique moment.'

And it wasn't an exaggeration. They felt as if they had inherited the world for that afternoon. Mickey Smith was tingling. He had succeeded in something that most surfers vaguely dream about but never realize: he had identified a wave that nobody knew about. And he knew from Rusty Long's reaction that it was comparable to some of the better waves out there. They all knew. Smith and Dan Skajarowski's older brother Steph had spent winter after winter in Tahiti. McCarthy and Blount had surfed Pipeline in Hawaii and they knew that this wave bore comparison. And then the backdrop: the dizzying canvas of the Cliffs of Moher made it otherworldly beautiful. This was no mere beach wave.

They could have made a pact there and then. They could have decided to keep it to themselves and maybe allow one or two more of their closest friends in as part of a covenant. After all, the wave had been breaking in splendid isolation for ever. The chances were that nobody would find it for years.

'A few people knew it was there,' Bill Keane, a veteran of the Clare surfing scene, contends. 'Boz [Paul Boswell, a local surfer] and those guys had spotted it and knew it was a great wave. But this was in the 1980s: we couldn't get our act together to go surf Crab Island. The attitude was: would you bother your arse going down a 700-foot cliff to go surf a crazy-looking fucking thing that wasn't possible anyway with the equipment we had then? We just left it alone.' But if any locals did know about it, then it was just a handful.

They surfed until it began to get dark. Robin Kent decided he would paddle across to the pier so that Dave Blount wouldn't have to make so many taxi trips on the jet-ski. 'Then, of course, we couldn't find him,' Blount recalls. 'It's pretty hard to find someone in the water when the light isn't good. It took us about ten minutes to spot him, then it took us another half hour to get the jet-ski on to the pier because the waves were so big.'

It had been a momentous day, but when Blount looks back on it, it is with a surfer's rather than a historian's heart. Having been among the first group to surf Aileen's never really meant that much to him. 'Ah. Pure dumb luck. If you ask me would I rather be the guy who was there when it was surfed first or the guy who surfed it better later on, I would rather be him. I don't attach much significance to it myself. I think Mickey should and would because he saw it fresh and, like he did with the wave at Riley's, he had this leap of imagination and wanted to figure out how to do it. With me, I felt I was following a bit on the coat tails because he had already planted that seed.'

Still, for a while that night they were the only people in the world who knew about the wave. Within weeks it would eclipse the fame of Moher itself. Even now Smith wishes that they could have kept it quiet for a bit longer. 'Maybe for a little while,' he says wistfully. 'Would have been nice to have it just to ourselves for a small while.'

They returned to Lahinch that evening elated. In Kenny's

pub they began to talk about what they had just been through. It didn't take long before word went round. 'John was buzzin' about the idea of this wave being on our doorstep,' Smith says. 'At that point in his life he was a party animal and he was on this crazy mission. He is a different dude now. He is just so mellow. I mean, he is still John: he is excitable. But back then he was just blown away that we had this wave and it became a local legend straight away. There were other guys around and they were thinking: right, I'll have a crack at this.' Like any wave worth its salt, it needed a name. A dense library of Celtic myths is associated with the Cliffs of Moher and the most fabulous of them all gave the cliff face at Aill Na Searrach (the 'Leap of the Foals') its name. It was there that seven foals, believed to be the guise the Tuatha De Danann had taken after St Patrick introduced religion to Ireland, became disorientated by the bright sunlight after hiding out in the Kilcornan Caves and galloped over the cliff face. The wave became Aileen's.

Once word had spread after that night in Kenny's, one by one surfers in the area went to investigate. 'The bush telegraph went into overdrive,' Tom Doidge-Harrison laughs now. 'Everyone was curious about this thing.'

When Doidge-Harrison showed up for the next proper swell Mickey Smith was at the cliffs, kicking about the fringes of the breakers on his surfboard, taking pictures. They hadn't properly met before that day. Doidge-Harrison had surfed around the world but he was completely taken aback by the size and ferocity of the waves. Straight away, fate conspired. He wasn't long in the water when an unholy set came in and he was perfectly placed to paddle in. Smith, as ever, had positioned himself to take a photograph from the most advantageous position. The image is placed among a montage in the shed where Doidge-Harrison shapes boards, and it isn't much bigger than a postcard. 'Don't worry, I have it blown up as well,' he says. 'Look, that was bloody huge. It was the biggest wave I had ever paddled into.'

On his very first day, Doidge-Harrison learned most of what he needed to know about the temperament of the break at Aileen's. Being in the right spot was crucial, and it wasn't that difficult to identify. 'But putting yourself there is hard because you have to convince yourself to sit there right where the action is going to be, and if you get it wrong, you pay. Shortly after I caught that wave, I got held under by two waves and broke a rib. So you have a moment of glory followed by pain quite rapidly. That's how it goes, isn't it?'

Smith also discovered the volatile side of the wave when he finally laid down the camera to enjoy himself. 'Three perfect days that October. Just flawless, big waves,' he says. It was late afternoon, golden sky beginning to fade, and he was paddling on his own. By now he was getting used to the pure enchantment of the place and felt as if he was getting to know the character of the waves too. The waves that came through that afternoon were frighteningly perfect: a true winter swell driving in from the far side of the Atlantic and forming with perfect direction into the most inviting barrels he had ever seen. But they were huge, beyond anything he had seen. He waited and waited until a sensational set came through. He kept his eye trained as the latest wave began to form and for a few seconds he could pretend that it was his prey. Then he paddled in.

'Just fell down the face and got completely hit by the lip with a force I have never, ever felt before. I was sent in a cartwheel up into the air. Both my fins were just snapped off my board and my wetsuit was ripped down my back. Then I was going down into the water really violently and got spat out the back of the wave. I got a breath, and then it pulled me back down again.' If Smith had discovered he was being attacked by a school of sharks he wouldn't have been surprised. 'I was completely disorientated. It turned out I had whiplash from the force on my back. But my board was somehow still attached to me and that is the only way that I knew where the surface was. I pulled at the leash. I had only one arm working at this stage, the other was completely dead. So I got back up to the surface and got my breath and turned around just in time to see the next wave coming down on me. When I got back into the channel, I just thought: fuckin' hell. This wave doesn't like me very much.'

Nobody knew what to expect. When Tom Gillespie showed up a few weeks later it was a mellow sunny day and the wave looked sparkling and inviting. It was slightly smaller than it had been the first day. The trio of Australian bodyboarders were already out there when Gillespie walked down the goats' trail for the first time. 'This was the first time I had ever even seen professional bodyboarders. And I was walking down the goats' trail just shitting it. I knew I was probably able for it but I couldn't be certain. So I paddled out and the first thing I see is Brenden Newton dropping down in front of me. For me, it was all a bit of a fantasy: like paddling into a surfing film. And at the same time it was beginning to really register with me that Ireland had this wave. So I was very nervous and careful . . . I remember watching to see who was inside me to make sure I wasn't dropping in on someone or making some stupid mistake. And then I got barrelled on my very first wave there. It was a fluke. But that is what happened.'

News about Aileen's now really began to travel. It hadn't been surfed more than a dozen times but it was an irresistible story: a giant wave at the foot of Ireland's most celebrated beauty spot and a vagabond group of surfers out there in winter. A story about the first party to surf was published in *Carve*. Soon, tales about its discovery began to appear in mainstream publications which generally ignored surfing. A lengthy story appeared in the London *Independent* under the audacious headline 'How the Perfect Surfer's Wave Was Conquered'.

'There was effort put in to getting to that level of exposure,' Blount says. 'It sold itself with a bit of a push. The *Independent* article went into a bit of a row that developed over how the Irish guys were treated. There was a bit of a falling-out . . . It comes back to the ego that is in every surfer. Not just big wave surfers but in everyone. In the *Carve* magazine spread there were just a few token shots of the Irish guys and John Mac [McCarthy] would have felt that we were as good as some of the English guys there. So there was a bit of a row and I waded in as well with a few broadsides. It is the only thing I felt bad about. It was a shitty time and it is the only thing I regret about the whole discovery of that wave, that little bit of aggravation. It did sort itself out and it is kind of petty and irrelevant. But it is funny because the whole media thing and egos are a real part of the surfing scene in Ireland, particularly the big wave stuff and the tow-in stuff. Like, there is a classic quote that one of Mickey's buddies came out with once: he said it was like people were rushing out of the water to get shots in time for the *Irish Times*. And that does still exist to varying degrees.'

Aileen's drew comparisons with the Jaws wave in Hawaii. Then in 2008 the Irish film maker Joel Conroy directed *Waveriders*, which was both an ethereal portrait of the emerging big wave surf culture in Ireland and a dramatic account of the life and times of George Freeth. The approach was bold and original, and as well as featuring well-known local surfers like Richard Fitzgerald from Bundoran and Easkey Britton from Rossnowlagh, the documentary contained footage of Kelly Slater, the preternaturally talented Floridian with Hollywood appeal, turning arabesques in stone-coloured Irish waters. Not only that, Slater spoke glowingly about wanting to come and surf in Ireland. Much like Kevin Naughton (who also appears in the documentary), he was attracted not just by the quality of the waves but by the opportunity to surf in a way that was becoming increasingly elusive: by himself.

That same year a television advertisement for one of the main Irish banks was framed around a breathtaking short film of a surfer at Aileen's. It was a clever move to ally the clause-and-contract environment of finance with beautifully captured images of a lone untethered surfer under the majestic cliffs – a world entirely removed from the polished interior of any bank. The surfer in the film was John McCarthy. Mickey Smith captured much of the close-up film, bobbing in the wave with a hand-held camera. It was one of those rare instances of advertising where the imagery never grows tired. You could watch it again and again, and the message was so subtle. Indeed there was no sell, except perhaps that as a customer of this bank you too could achieve this sense of freedom and adventure – you'd never feel as if you were being huckstered. Even as the commercial was being broadcast the walls of the Irish property market were dissolving and hundreds of thousands of people were beginning to understand that they faced decades of being locked into punitive mortgage agreements. But still, the short film seemed to catch the zeitgeist, with its slow-motion shots of frigid waves and forbidding cliffs. Irish surfing, with its promise of bracingly healthy sessions in the Atlantic followed by après-surf in turf-smoked pubs, had become a fashionable lifestyle choice by 2008. The sight of cars crowded with young professionals and zipped-up boards on roof-racks gravitating towards the surf towns in the west of Ireland was no longer confined to the summer months.

While the commercial seemed stirringly new and arresting, it was actually the latest in a rich tradition. Surfing had caught the eyes of the ad men even when it was an underground pursuit in Ireland. As far back as 1981 Guinness commissioned a television commercial that may well have contained the most risqué images ever transmitted by the national broadcaster. The opening shot of a flaming sunset segued into the most azure waters imaginable, and panned across sun-kissed sand populated only by bikini-clad girls, one of whom was filmed with her back to the television audience, taking pictures with a camera and wearing bikini bottoms that rode scandalously below the hip. Then the action moved towards the waves, where tanned surfers in bright shorts bombed and dived through the surf and enjoyed spectacular wipe-outs, and in one case ramped up the face of the wave so that the momentum lifted him free of his board and he flew for a few seconds before falling back into the sea in perfect synchronicity with the wah-wah guitar riff composed by Bill Whelan (who would go on to write the score for *Riverdance*). Towards the end of the commercial, the gushing water merged with the creamy stout forming in the pint glass, and it ended with the baritone advice, 'Move over to Guinness.'

The commercial was more or less forgotten in the decades afterwards but has in recent years turned up on YouTube, that wonderful junkyard of television nostalgia. Even now it depicts an idealized lifestyle; when it was originally screened thirty-plus years ago it must have seemed unbearably exotic and foreign. This was just a year after the Boomtown Rats' scathing pop comment 'Banana Republic' reached number one in the charts. In March 1981 Bobby Sands led the hunger strikes in the Maze and in Long Kesh; by May he was dead. The political scene was reduced to a stark battle between Charles Haughey and Garret Fitzgerald. So the advert was pure escapism, and literally a black joke. Very few could up and leave for those tropical waters. Travel was prohibitively expensive: two weeks in Gran Canaria in May 1981 cost 239 punt per person. Foreign holidays were little more than rumours, exotic sprees that such-and-such went on. The sand in that commercial was not Irish sand and those tropical waters did not belong to Ireland. And surfing was still more or less an invisible sport in Ireland, regarded as the preserve of hippies or moneyed folk with a radical streak. Yet the commercial was not attempting to sell some dubious new foreign lager but Flann O'Brien's pint of plain, the drink sacred to men in peaked caps. Whether it was because the idea was so preposterous or the imagery so eye-catching, it worked. Four years later the Clare folk singer Christy Moore released a tremendously successful album, *Ordinary Man*. Among the most quoted lyrics was the refrain from 'Delirium Tremens': 'As I sat looking up at the Guinness ad I could never figure out / How yer man stayed up on the surfboard after fourteen pints of stout.'

As Guinness went on to produce even more imaginatively daring adverts in the decades that followed, surfing was a recurrent theme, most memorably in the 1990s offering which featured charging waves transforming into rearing wild horses. By then Ireland no longer seemed to be the last outpost of surfing. Magazines had begun to appear on newsagents' shelves and it was possible for those who were interested to learn a thing or two about the legendary surfing breaks in Hawaii and southern California. But that 1990s advert still leaned towards the fabulous, with its emphasis on make-believe and legend.

When the Aileen's advert was made eighteen years later, the surfing it showcased was stark and beautiful and completely authentic. The way surfing was portrayed had come full circle from that dreamy, faintly surreal advert in 1981. 'It came out that Christmas,' McCarthy says, remembering his debut. 'I don't have a television but my mother used to call me every time it was on. I know that it used to feature on Six Nations rugby afternoons. Ireland did well that year so a lot of people seemed to notice it. And as a kid, that would have been my ultimate dream. I used to lie in bed as a child holding the board above my head in the air pretending I was flying through a wave. And here I was on television.' His face lights up as he gives a skittish laugh.

In his teenage years and throughout his twenties McCarthy was one of the best-known surfers on the Irish scene. Now he is in his mid-thirties, a slender man with an impossibly open, warm face, fizzing with good health and an attitude to life that defies handy categorization. On the surface, the narrative of his life seems enviable: everything came easily and he just seemed to skate through on a combination of charm, intelligence and, like any good surfer, the instinctive knowledge of when to make his move. Even now, in the teeth of the most vicious recession in the history of the state, the surf shop and school that he runs in Lahinch is one of the most demonstrable examples of the popularity of wave riding. McCarthy knows that from the outside it has always looked as if life granted him a comfortable seat, and that he should pop up to appear in this primetime advertisement seemed to confirm this. 'You know, Fergal [Smith] was my stunt double for the advert,' McCarthy volunteers. 'It was a miracle I was in it at all because they filmed him as much as they did me and Fergal is that much a better surfer than I am. Technically, it was difficult. They had to wait a full year before the wave even broke properly so there was a chance it might never have happened.'

McCarthy's profile in Irish surfing and the fact that he was among the group that pioneered Aileen's made him an obvious candidate when the film makers were scouting around for someone to feature in the commercial. He grew up in Tramore, was coached by Hugh O'Brien Moran, and was something of a local prodigy. His ascension in the professional world seemed as smooth as his facility with surfing; McCarthy managed to trade what the college brochures would call an 'exciting career' in information technology, which took him to Japan and Germany, for an equally successful life in Lahinch: he set up his business just before the vogue for Irish surfing weekends took off. He is grateful for all that and he feels blessed by everything.

When we met on one of those spitting west-of-Ireland summer afternoons, McCarthy and his wife, Rebecca, were preparing for parenthood. As he spoke about his life as a surfer, about the person he had been when the sport was his main focus in life, it was in the warm, slightly mystified tone of talking about someone he was fond of but had never fully known. 'Surfing has probably been among the top two or three influences in my life. But when I was younger, surfing was my identity. As a young man, you are looking for ways to carve out your name: to be significant or to be somebody. So when I was living in Frankfurt I was just another computer guy: I was nobody. But then I came back to Lahinch and I was a surfer. So you feel as if you are someone!'

Surfing shaped precisely who he was when he was too young to fully understand. At thirteen, just three years after he took up the sport, he was selected for Irish teams and won national championships at junior and senior level. Together with Dave Blount he flew the flag for Tramore surfing. He was an automatic selection for Irish teams after that, coasted through college, and found himself living in Tokyo, young and affluent, surfing in the Sendai area at weekends. Living the dream! When the tsunami hit the region in 2011 he recalled being in an Irish pub in some multi-storey building years earlier. He remembered a sudden jolt, 'like being in a lift that drops an inch suddenly'. There was quiet for a second, a collective pause, and then the glasses began tinkling and the laughter returned and everyone forgot about it.

Whether in Japan or Germany, McCarthy had it arranged so that he could take a couple of months in the winter and go off to surf somewhere balmy and far away, maybe Africa or Hawaii. Even though his job was demanding he was able to maintain a standard, winning a bronze medal at the European Championships as recently as 2006. He had this sunny way about him and people warmed to him. He enjoyed being John McCarthy. How could he not?

The one problem was that it was all a bit of a blur. He felt this hollowness and he couldn't locate its centre. When he was around thirty he was in Hawaii, familiar with the scene now, an habitué of an experience the global stampede of back-packers get to do once and then tick off the list as proof that their carefree side is intact. 'I was past the go-drinking-with-the-backpackers thing. You know, who do I hang around with now? What do I do now? So I started asking these questions. And I think it was probably then that I began to look a bit deeper into what I was about.'

He began exploring what he now calls the 'Eastern stuff', and started to practise yoga. That led him to other religions. One afternoon he bought a Bible in Sydney almost without thinking about it and started to read. He has never stopped. Over the coming months and years, it was as if a fog began to clear. 'Surfing is always going to be a big part of my life but I began to see that it wasn't the answer. I thought it was every-thing and I can see now that I was definitely searching for something. When you are trying to create who you are, when you are trying to find out who the hell you are, you do things like that. When you meet God you suddenly understand your purpose for being on the planet. And it makes sense: there is a rest in your soul. In the book of Ecclesiastes, there is a passage where Solomon comes to the understanding that it is all grasping after the wind. Whether it is knowledge, fame, women, honour, riches: it is all just grasping after the wind. It is here and then it is gone.'

One day in Lahinch McCarthy met a member of the Christian Surfers. McCarthy vaguely knew of the organization and had seen representatives showing up at surf contests down the years. He had them down as harmless oddballs, and the notion of surfers with a holy bent amused him. At that time he was returning to Christianity in his own way. Making deals with God, as the song goes. He would show up for Mass on Sunday morning, privately celebrating that his friends were in bed with screaming hangovers and reasoning that his presence gave him a moral edge on them. He began talking with the Christian Surfer and out of curiosity agreed to attend a conference in Devon. He felt a little bit ridiculous trekking down to southern England just to meet a bunch of surfers who wanted to talk about Christianity. But he wasn't going to miss it.

When he arrived, he walked into a marquee on the Friday evening and was taken aback by what he encountered. It was a bit like *Point Break* meets *Jesus Christ Superstar*. 'All these surf dudes playing guitar and waving their hands in the air,' McCarthy grins. 'It felt a bit full on to me. I didn't think I needed that. My feeling at the time was that life should be about "being good". But what I didn't know at the time was that it wasn't about being good along your own standards. We are all sinners, and that is what it comes down to. So I went back to Devon for a second time a few months later in the knowledge that my attempts at being good had failed. That there were things I was doing that were offensive to God. I was saying: I need Your help here. Things had started to affect me.'

Everything hinged on that day. He rattles the date out without hesitation: 23 July 2006. After that he was committed. Abruptly he ended the lifestyle pattern that had taken him from adolescence through the haze of his twenties. 'The pubs, running after girls, getting smashed drunk: all that stuff just stopped for me. My personality wasn't different but my life changed radically. As a friend said to me: reality just got a whole lot more real. I don't think I have been drunk since that point.'

In some ways his experience as a surfer – the adherence to ritual – helped him. But he also began to strip down his attitude to the sport that had been at the epicentre of his life. He made himself understand why surfing was so important to him. It was about the adrenalin and the uncomplicated joy of the waves, but there was also something else. Surfing fed his ego. His reputation was like a shield that he could carry with him. When he thinks back to the person he was at the turn of the millennium, he remembers always looking for acclamation.

'The trick about surfing is that it is completely selfish. You are doing it for yourself. And that is fine: it is the same with athletes. But with surfing it is all about the addiction of chasing the next big wave, and hopefully it will be better than the last one. So, for instance, you have this wave Aileen's and you are in this Colosseum of a barrel and then you come through it and you get this adrenalin rush and it is the ultimate high of highs. Then photographs might arrive and you get a mad ego rush. And you show the shots to your friends, and you show them again, and eventually they are saying, "OK John! I've seen it! You've shown me how great you are." That's how it was with me seven years ago. For me to have a photographer like Mickey Smith take a photo of me and for it to make some cover: I would have felt as though that made me complete. But what I learned is: you are on your own. You can't hold on to that high. None of these things happens to you. Only God can satisfy the desires of the soul. That is my view. The ego is not gone. I'm still working on it. But it shouldn't define my life any more. I am seeking to do God's will, but when a swell comes up there is that issue of whether he wants me to be out there or not.'

The suddenness of McCarthy's change in direction took friends and acquaintances aback. He still goofed around and he looked the same, but when the weekend came he was conspicuous by his absence. About a year after his conversion he walked into Flanagan's pub and his friends were there, just as he had left them. The moment was in itself like something from one of those sophisticated alcohol commercials. His friends pressed him into having a drink and someone handed him a shot of tequila. For a few seconds he wavered. He felt as if he missed the old life: the fun and mindlessness of getting goosed and letting Friday night carry you through until Sunday. Then he walked out the door. 'My heart just wasn't in it. I felt as if everything was going well at that moment and I just didn't want to leave that feeling.'

Things weren't without their tough moments. He took

no joy in explaining to his mother that he was going to get baptized for the second time in his life. And she asked him, not unreasonably, 'John, what is wrong with the way that you were brought up?' But people got used to it. The friends that he grew up with are still his friends. At a wedding not so long ago he fell into conversation with a guy he has known for donkey's years. 'This would be a hard man. He wouldn't be into talking about God. But he says to me: I can see this has been good for you.'

He met Rebecca when he was invited to give a talk at a Christian Union meeting at University College Cork. They live in Lahinch these days, and although McCarthy is constantly in the water giving surfing lessons to tourists and novices, he has become ambivalent about chasing bigger waves since they learned that Rebecca was expecting their child. Dave Blount is still his favourite person to go surfing with. McCarthy readily admits to having been wary of bigger waves until his mid-teens. Even after he began surfing junior contests for Ireland he remained an average swimmer. It was always Blount who egged him on, and when they visited Waimea Bay at twenty-one, something clicked. 'Even the housewives were out on the big waves over there. It was about going outside the comfort zone.'

These days he finds himself drawn to that place less and less. He never wants to go out with Blount unless he is certain that he can match his friend's enthusiasm and intensity for the experience. Blount astounds him: he is as absorbed by surfing now as he was when they were both teenagers. And McCarthy has to know that he is completely in tune with his friend – that he can be there for him – if they are towing into powerful waves. He feels he has been as lucky as a black cat down the years, with no near misses to report. He has been with surfers who have resurfaced on the water bug-eyed and breathless but has never known what that feels like. Not so long ago he encountered a base jumper at the Cliffs of Moher. McCarthy was stupefied by the recklessness of this guy's plan: to hurl himself over the edge and release his chute with just enough time to prevent him from hitting the rocks below. 'I was looking at him and I said, "Do you know that you could be about to die?" And he said, "Well, you surf big waves. You have gotten away with it all your life." And you know, surfing bigger waves gradually means you can justify it in your mind. But is it dangerous? Yeah, it is super dangerous. Young men do stupid things. And I'm not sure where I am with it right now.'

The last time he had a memorable day at the cliffs he wasn't even on a surfboard. He had a few hours to himself and it was a sunny afternoon and he crossed the fields and sat there for half an hour. There literally wasn't a sinner around. For once he wasn't fixating on tides or lugging a surfboard down the trail or narrowing his focus until there was nothing but the sea involved. He saw the place as it had been when the Tuatha De Dannan used to roam the same heights. 'For me, it is about that word "creation",' McCarthy says earnestly. 'The beauty of the place, you know. It hits you. It is an escape.'

But he is quietly proud that his other escape, the one that propelled him through his teenage years and into adulthood, has somehow found a means of expression on that wave beneath the cliffs. He is probably too modest about his own place in Irish surfing. 'I had probably tried about forty different sports when I came to surfing and it quickly became an addiction for me rather than a decision. I wasn't great or anything but I was the best of the bunch. When you look at Fergal and Cain Kilcullen and those guys now, they are at a different level. And I watched young Gearóid McDaid surf not so long ago. He might become the best Irish surfer ever.'

He has seen a few contenders come and go down the years. When McCarthy started off, wetsuits fell somewhere between expensive necessity and outright luxury: owning one was a big deal. During the days when fathers and sons crowd his shop in Lahinch waiting to get fitted out, part of him still marvels that the sport has become so popular. There is no question that some of his customers were alerted to him and to the thrill of surfing after seeing that television commercial and he is candid about the fact that the Aileen's advert has helped all five surf schools in Lahinch enormously. He enjoys it, and still shakes his head when he sees how busy the beach becomes with fledgling surfers on sunny days. There was a time when he could never have imagined Irish surfing ever leaving the fringes.

These days, though, when the sea turns baleful and the sky seems to fall in on Clare, McCarthy is often content to light the fire, secure in the knowledge that a handful of lads are flinging boards off some reef not so far away. He can't really say what it is all about but he comforts himself with the vague notion that there is a greater hand at work. And he has a theory. 'I trust that God has a plan for all these surfers in the same way as he had the fishermen of two thousand years ago. He uses the foolish things to confound the wise. I know that God is doing something special here and I haven't a clue what it is. His ways are higher. I hope when I am seventy or so I will understand. But I think that Aileen's wave is part of what God is doing.'

When Kevin Naughton was a teenager, his idol was an Australian surfer named Peter Troy. Troy's father had served Australia in World War Two, and his son was born in wartime; his relentless pursuit of a lighter existence might be seen as a response to the darkness of that period. Troy was both charmed and charming and travelled compulsively, surfing in 138 countries and mingling effortlessly with beach bums and high society. Someone once took a photograph of Troy along the way in which he is sitting on the roadside in the sunshine in regulation checked shirt, blond hair pushed to one side, surfboard under one arm and suitcase by his side. He is thumbing a lift to somewhere. That was the picture that caught Naughton's eye. 'That is who I wanted to be. That is who I wanted to emulate. He wasn't big into contests or what-ever. And it is funny . . . I sometimes get compared to him in articles now and I smile when I see our names in the same sentence because he is the reason that I wanted to do it.'

Troy and Naughton and all the others who came afterwards were just following the same instinctive urge as that which gripped the most famous water adventurer of them all: like Huckleberry Finn, they lit out. And tens of thousands followed.

A couple of years ago, Gregory Schell put together a documentary of the trips Naughton and Peterson made entitled *The Far Shore*. Naughton had taken a Super 8 camera with him and the footage he captured is a precious visual document of a kind of wandering that is no longer possible. The mood in those flickering films is, as Naughton says, illuminated by a kind of blissful innocence. The duo have also been working on the series of articles they wrote all those years ago, editing and reviewing them for a book.

'Nostalgia's a great thing,' Naughton laughs.

In 2006 he met up with the original band who started surfing the Irish Atlantic forty years earlier for a reunion that was wonderfully captured in *The Silver Surfari*, a documentary by Naomi Britton. It, too, was an unabashed exercise in nostalgia, but more importantly it was a celebration of the daftly romantic streak that compelled them to give this strange and exotic sport a try. They retraced old roads from Lahinch up as far as Rossnowlagh, and the evidence that surfing is no longer a cult pursuit in Ireland was all around them. Naughton has visited Ireland frequently enough to have seen some of the up-and-coming surfers. He remembers the excitement he felt one day when he watched Cain Kilcullen surfing: the immediate recognition that here was an Irish lad who would easily distinguish himself in the waters of Huntington. And like thousands of others, he watched the footage of Fergal Smith on that azure wave in Cloudbreak. 'It was great to see that. You know, when I was first surfing around Bundoran and Sligo, they could well have been in prams on the promenade.'

The period when Naughton felt as if he was the only surfer in Ireland is gone. Even then he knew it was a temporary luxury: the waves were just too good to remain unexplored. When he is in the northwest now, he invariably finds himself driving out to Bundoran just to see how the Peak is faring. 'But like all the good breaks, it's busy. It looks just as crowded as Trestles [off California] on a lot of days.'

That insatiable search for yet another untapped, never-seen-before wave hasn't left him either. He still goes on treks, driving down lanes in the hope that maybe some unnoticed corner of the west coast has been secreting a last great wave. He takes consolation in the possibility that the islands have yet to be fully explored but he knows that day is coming too. Ireland has followed the same pattern as everywhere else. 'It's never going to go back to what it was like in the 1970s. The genie is out of the bottle.'

3

An Elemental Pull

So this wave, then, drew a handful of them to Clare as if it possessed magnetic qualities. Picture the coastline from Doolin on any evening from November to March when the winding roads have a blue sheen and the sky and sea seem to merge and then imagine this tribe nestled into the more obscure corners of the land.

At Tom Doidge-Harrison's house, not far from Kilshanny, you can stand at the back door and see half the county when the sky is clear. You would never find the house except for the front half of a surfboard which Tom has attached to a telephone pole pointing towards the side-road-off-a-side-road that leads there. The trademark initials that adorn any board he shapes – an unmistakable slanted *dh* – have faded a little through the seasons but are still recognizable. He isn't fully certain where the unusual double-barrelled name originates. Harrison is a solid Yorkshire name and as far as he knows the

Doidge lineage is Cornish. As a boy he heard several stories as to how the name was acquired: that his grandfather was orphaned and was adopted by a family named Doidge, and also that he had a falling out with his family and went to live with cousins of that name. The only place he has ever seen it is in a phone book in Cornwall. But through his skill as a board-shaper he is making the name more popular than it has ever been.

When you follow the direction of that improvised sign, you cross a humped bridge over a stream and then begin to climb and climb and at the very top of the road is the stone-cut cottage that Harrison spotted when he moved to Clare over a decade ago. He has converted an adjacent shed into a work room where he shapes surfboards for some of the best surfers in the country. He spends about ten months of the year shaping boards and devotes the other two to his primary profession: he is a mining engineer.

'The mines are perfect places for surfers to work,' he mused one indolent evening, happily tired after an afternoon surfing at Aileen's. Harrison is thirty-five and greyhound athletic with a mop of curls, and though he was born in Cambridge and lived all over the south of England, he has travelled so much it is hard to categorize him as any nationality. 'I met quite a few surfers in mines in Australia over the years. The nature of the job suits them perfectly because they work for a block of time and then head off to the coast and surf for the summer.'

He has managed to establish the same pattern for himself. One December night about five years ago Harrison left Kilshanny for one of his occasional mining trips. All he knew was that he was headed for Russia. He took a flight from Shannon to London (at a time when 'connectivity' was the word most associated with the Shannon region) on a Sunday night and finally reached his destination, a remote gold mine in Nezhdaninskoye, on the Thursday night. By then he was disorientated with tiredness. His flight from London to Moscow had been delayed, after which he'd had a twelve-hour wait in the Russian capital for his next flight to Yakutsk. By the time he reached there his luggage had been lost and he had faint hopes of ever seeing it again. 'I stepped outside the door of the main terminal into a minus forty evening wearing jeans and trainers,' he laughs. 'Had to go around the petrol stations buying underwear.'

After a brief meeting with his hosts he set off on what was the longest and strangest journey of his life: an eighteen-hour trek in a six-wheel jeep across a frozen empty landscape, a trip he shared with five perfect strangers. It was at once fascinating and monotonous. Everything was frigid. They drove across river surfaces which had become channels of crushed ice and on roads which stretched for miles, and on which they were the only moving thing. 'The rivers looked like glaciers,' he explained, before breaking his thoughts to trace the path of a kestrel across the mellow Clare evening with a forefinger. 'Look at that fella! Yeah, so every now and again the road would fork and with no signposts the driver had to guess which way to go and often the roads just turned into dead ends.' Only his translator spoke English so most of the journey passed in silence, the only language used the international one of sympathetic glances and shared chocolate. He was there to act as an observer for the exploration of an old state mine.

The Russians literally wanted to find gold in the hills. But Harrison was wondering if he would even survive the drive. 'It was bonkers. I think we passed through one town the entire time. The land was flat as far as you could see for hours and then we were through mountains which were like being in the Alps. And it was incredibly cold. The whole experience was just very weird. I have never done anything like it in my life.'

When they finally reached the mine it was populated by a hundred souls. Eleven locomotive engines stacked in a row powered the entire plant. JCBs were used to tip coal into a furnace which kept the heating and water system going. Alcohol was forbidden on the camp. There were no televisions. In the winter, people played ping-pong or they read or they slept; in the summer, they hunted or fished. 'People were basically living there and they were really well paid so they were sending money back to wherever. But they were all really, really lovely. And the thing that I got a blast from was that the women there were treated really respectfully. Normally mines have a fairly tough macho atmosphere but the women there were just revered and that surprised me.'

Harrison spent three weeks at the mine, navigating a tunnel network decorated with extraordinary stalagmites and stalactites that seemed as precious to him as the hidden metal itself. Nights were tedious: he went to bed at ten, woke bright as a button at one in the morning and spent the rest of the night just listening to the sounds of winter in the Russian outback. If during those hours he narrowed down his reasons for being there, surfing was at the heart of them. Whether by accident or design, he had chosen a profession that enabled him to work in intense bursts and then devote more time to the water and to crafting boards. As well as working in mines across Australia, Harrison has spent several months in northern Chile, near the San José mine which would become a source of worldwide fascination in 2010. In Ireland he works at the Lisheen mine near Thurles for several weeks every year.

His wife, Raquel, is Spanish. She doesn't surf but understands the draw he feels to these turbulent spots on the Atlantic. The couple had a daughter less than a year ago so both Raquel and Nora are part of these conversations he has with himself whenever he tries to articulate why he needs to surf. 'I wouldn't say it is an obsession,' he says slowly. 'It is just the thing I do, and I get cranky when I don't. I guess the only other sport that you could compare it to is mountaineering. But then mountaineering always has the summit as a final goal where surfing doesn't. You are just repeating it! Raquel is happy for me to go if I don't take liberties all the time. And I suppose if it wasn't for surfing we might be living in a lovely sunny Spanish city rather than on a hill in Clare. And this place is great when it is sunny but in winter the wind and rain can be incessant and that's tough. But this is the longest that I have ever lived in one place for.'

He had plenty of time to muse on such issues in Russia. The job was completed, but there was a low point: a bizarre argument he had with a colleague through his translator. The exchange lacked the quickfire retorts and interruptions of any normal row; instead it was punctuated by angry outbursts in two foreign tongues and then patient explanations by the translator, who became upset. 'It was awful because it was all just a misunderstanding and all three of us were friends by then. So I felt bad about it. But that was towards the end. I had to leave on a very specific date or I was going to miss the last flight back to Moscow before Christmas. I just made it and was home in Clare by 22 December.'

And that's what happens in this community. People are surfing one day and then they drop out of sight for weeks or months on end. It is a loose and casual fraternity. Bill Keane lives in a cottage on the hills above Doolin and he offers his visitors the most brilliant set of directions ever: 'So at those crossroads, go right. Then keep going. You'll go past the turn to Doolin. You'll see Mac's petrol station. Stop there. Go in. Buy a packet of biscuits. Then head on about half a mile and take the next left . . .'

On a misty August afternoon Keane was working on surf-boards in his shed and listening to Lyric FM at full volume. He put on the kettle, and after making coffee stared unhappily at the soft rain falling against the window pane. It had been a summer of nothingness, humid damp days and calm waters, and Keane had a caged-animal impatience about him as he talked about surfing. 'I am hanging out here since April and that was the last decent swell,' he sighs. 'Summer has been a fucking write-off. Things are starting to pick up. Bits and pieces, a few waves. Nothing classical. It is frustrating some-times to think that you are giving it all up for waves that don't come.'

In the specific sense, 'it' means a gallop to somewhere sunnier. In the general sense, it means the more conventional lifestyle he decided against so he could surf more. Keane was born in 1970, which makes him young enough to still surf well and old enough to have a clear recollection of when Ireland was a different country. He is both laid back and sharp as a pin in his observations, and even though surfing nurtured his wanderlust spirit, he was at hand to observe the surfing movement becoming what it is now. He was fourteen when he first started surfing: it was St Stephen's Day 1984 and he got a board from the Shannon Outdoor Club and no sooner had he taken hold of it than something fundamental occurred to him: 'Nobody could tell you what the rules were and you didn't have to wait for anyone else.'

That was it. He started surfing off the beach in Lahinch and gradually grew bold enough to try the waves off the reefs at Cregg and Spanish Point. On his bedroom wall he kept a poster of the 1972 European Surf Championships that were held in Lahinch. He thought of it then as a quaint memento of the belle époque of Irish surfing when moustachioed demi-gods from the Continent visited the West to thrill lads and lassies alike with their virtuoso performances. When Keane was a teenager the surfing movement was in a lull. And he loved that: it gave him the sense of participating in something decadent and, most importantly, entirely his. He fell into the company of the maybe half a dozen guys who appeared to be serious about nothing in life as much as surfing, guys like Brendan McGrath and Paul Boswell, from whom he learned a lot. Willie Britton would turn up sporadically and Keane found himself drawn to the effortless elegance with which the Donegal man surfed. 'He was very talented. Like Fergal [Smith] in that he was always very cool and calm. Quiet. You just knew that this guy knew what he was about and it was good to hang with someone who had his shit together.'

And even as he was learning the sport, Keane was beginning to figure out where surfing, so obscure in Ireland, fitted in the bigger picture. 'Remember *Sports Stadium?*' he asks suddenly, referencing the defunct RTÉ television magazine that was the scourge of rainy childhood Saturdays for three entire decades. 'Yeah? Well, I used to hate it. Racing, racing, racing. Dull as fuck. But there was this one afternoon when it was very stormy – floods throughout the country and nothing happening. All the horse racing was cancelled. And they showed this film called *Fall Line*, looking into the cross-over between boarding, surfing, hang gliding and skiing. And in the surfing section they showed Nat Young, the 1966 world champion. But there was this other guy who I thought was amazing. He was a goofy-footer – stands with his right foot forward and he was left-handed, as I am. So it is kind of like being ciotóg side [a left-handed hurler] in the surfing world. And I felt an affinity for this guy rather than Nat Young. This guy was from the outback in Oz and he fitted into that crock-of-shit category of soul surfing. But you knew that he was genuine and he was doing it for himself.'

And that was what Keane wanted to do. He formulated a plan: he did his apprenticeship as a carpenter, enabling him to work anywhere and at any time, and then just took off. Tahiti, Hawaii, the Pacific coast . . . he took himself where he pleased and by and large missed the dreariness of the late 1980s. Keane belonged to a generation of Irish people for whom emigration or stagnation were the predominant choices. But as he remembers, many people were just fine with the latter. As has been recently noted, the 1980s was the fun recession. 'People were on the dole and on the rock 'n' roll and were loving it,' he laughs.

His pattern was to return to Clare during the summer

months, work for a while, get some money together and dis-appear on his next jaunt. His twenties and then his thirties passed blissfully in that way. He has been slowly renovating the cottage he bought over a decade ago, which as it happens is just across the field from where his great-grandmother grew up. Now he is one of the senior men in a local surfing scene that has been transformed beyond his imagination, and he finds it thrilling. The advent of Aileen's and the wave at Riley's and the novelty of seeing the water at Lahinch crowded with novice and seasoned surfers delight him.

He is something of a librarian when it comes to surf culture and continues to read about the new international and Irish names coming through. He first came across Mickey Smith when he was surfing at Crab Island. 'Mickey was filming: he was actually there to film this bodyboarder that I happened to burn on this particular wave. I was in a tube and feeling happy with myself and looked up and saw this guy on a board point-ing a camera at me. I thought this was fantastic! And I wanted the photo cos never in my life did I have a photograph taken of me in a wave.'

He began talking with this polite, affable Englishman and they became friendly. Over the coming years he gradually got to know this new generation of surfers living around Clare. One morning a few winters ago he showed up at Crab Island to find Fergal Smith already there. 'It was one of those horrid sub-zero days and you are in bits after two hours in the water. If the water was two degrees, that was the height of it. This was at eight in the morning. So I went away and came back and Fergal was still there in that wetsuit surfing waves at six o'clock in the evening. Mickey was out there too. I wouldn't say that I know Mickey much at all but I do know that he has a fabulous eye and he has incredible patience when it comes to filming. There is nobody doing what those boys are doing anywhere in the world. The dedication they have for this is incredible. I think what they do is fucking bonkers. And it is also really admirable.'

Cars cruised up and down the short promenade at Strandhill all afternoon looking for a parking bay. It was a gorgeous July Friday and the Sligo resort seemed to shimmer in anticipation of a busy weekend. That seaside noise – summer wind, fifteen different radios playing the Don Henley classic, and gulls high above – was everywhere. At the Shells café, Seamus McGoldrick sat nibbling on a sandwich and saluting every second person who walked past. He is a local lad and everyone knows him, greeting him with a cheerful 'Well, Shambles' as they passed by. McGoldrick is twenty-six and boyish but can sound like a Civil War veteran when he charts the progress of his childhood village to the place it has become now. Loyalty to his home place is the main thing that has prevented him from moving to Clare, where he spends so much time it is a home-from-home.

'I wouldn't live anywhere else,' he states passionately. 'Strandhill has its dark side – it can be bloody depressing here in winter – but it is a good place, you know. It was over-developed and there was some dodgy planning here, no question. And thank God there are no ghost estates here but the place has become very money orientated. The whole surfing scene only really took off in the last ten years and people like to come down here and socialize now. It is great to be part of that and to see that happening. But you can be the cynic about it too.'

And then McGoldrick takes a look round and starts to demolish the teeming seascape so that it is restored to what it was when he started surfing eighteen years earlier: gone is the inevitable block of waterfront flats (with tiny balconies) and back to life comes the beautiful house that previously stood there, owned by the McDermott family, who 'minded' him after school when he was in fifth class. The McDermott boys surfed and they used to get changed in a shed next to the house. They ate cheese sandwiches for sustenance and it was generally cold and they had the entire beach to themselves. 'The McDermott boys got me into it. But my very first surf was at Coney Island with my two sisters and my mum. We bought the gear in Penny's in Sligo. See that guy there?' he says, pointing at a man strolling past in shorts. 'Well, that's my neighbour Alan, and when we started surfing we used to beg our families and the other neighbours to come and watch us. They never did though. I remember one afternoon five or six lads cowering in the rain watching us, but that was it for an audience.'

McGoldrick is a bodyboarder, and even if he had been the most preternaturally talented stand-up surfer in the Western world you have to fancy that he still would have opted to throw his lot in with bodyboarding if only to buck the trend. In the 1990s he wore out his parents' VCR watching *The Underground Tapes Volumes One and Two* featuring the most avant-garde bodyboarders on film. It looked to him like more fun than stand-up surfing and he was attracted to the fact that bodyboarding was regarded as the poor relation of wave riding. 'I think surfing has a lot to do with the male ego,' he declares. 'Phallic worship and all that. Honestly. The types that start fights and look for aggro: they are surfing types.' But when McGoldrick started learning his craft there was nobody to pick fights with. Strandhill was gloriously deserted on most days of the year.

He has torn into swells with kamikaze abandon on several continents, but the wave that gave him the lesson he carries with him was right here in Strandhill. A wintry day, the promenade ghostly, and he was out there bobbing on the water. His friends had packed it in and were back on the shore changing. As often happens, this was towards the end of a session and the waves seemed to reward him for his loyalty, arriving constantly and heavily. He hung on despite his hunger and despite the fading light and the fact that there was nobody out there with him. He wished for something special and mean, and a promising set duly arrived. He kept his eye on a big, lumbering, heavy-looking wave as it built and went to paddle into it. When he realized it wasn't happening and tried to pull back, he discovered that he had become part of the wave. He was fifteen years old and his skinny body had no argument to offer. He can't remember where he first read that expression 'over the falls' – used in the surf world to describe the sensation of being sucked up through the lip of a wave as it peaks and then slams towards the seabed – but at that moment he felt its full accuracy as he darted through the arc of the wave, hit the sand on the ocean floor and was pinned there. It might well have been a pair of nightclub bouncers holding him to the ground. 'And I was really struggling. I was very scared and I started to get woozy and then I had this vision of my doorbell going and the cops saying what they say about you to your parents when you are after drowning. It is all silent down there, and then when you get back up it is all whooooosh . . . just this explosion of noise.'

He was washed back into the shallows and then tumbled out, throwing up water and collapsing on the ground in front of his friends, who managed to contain their concern. 'They started laughing because I'd lain down beside this dead bird.' Once he got his breath back he went straight back into the water just to reassure himself that it was all right. Nothing as bad has happened since. 'I have had a few scrapes but that day taught me a lot. The funny thing is, when you come back up to the surface after a scare like that the first thing you think is: I'm packing in the fags. Then when you get back to dry land, the first thing you do is spark up. And it's the nicest smoke you could have!'

Even at that age, surfing was rewarding him. He was good enough to secure a place on the Irish team along with two other Strandhill men, Ross McDermott and Shane Meehan. There was a bit of glamour attached to that, even if he doesn't remember the contests as much as the fun. 'The usual. Getting caught drunk and that. When I first went on those European competitions it felt as if we were the backward Irish. I eventually figured that no one would notice if I finished first or not and that anyhow I couldn't beat these lighter guys. It was only in later years that I learned not to be daunted.'

McGoldrick was a bright boy: he sailed through the Leaving Certificate at sixteen and won a place at Trinity to study astrophysics. He knows there is an alternative Seamus McGoldrick out there somewhere in a laboratory coat. He has a friend from college who is in Lausanne working with the European Organization for Nuclear Research and he sometimes wonders what he might have done had he signed up for the PhD he was considering in his fourth year. 'I got a free education in Ireland for which I'm really grateful. But I studied science to find out what was going on in the world and by then I realized that it doesn't give you the answers.'

During his time at college he bumped into Tom and Fintan Gillespie at a local wave called Black Spot so he knew a few people in the city who were equally obsessed with surfing and who shared his anxiety whenever there was a swell in the west and they were stuck in the capital. But living in the city for four years was a strain. He felt trapped. So he left Dublin, went to France and ended up working in a nursing home. 'Thought about becoming a nurse, actually,' he says, musing on those messy post-college years. 'But I got fired. Then I missed a flight to Indonesia and wasn't getting any kind of refund. So I had to start saving again and eventually went over there in January 2007. Came back three months later. Went on the dole for six months. And I started strumming guitar. Then I did this music course in Drumshanbo in tin whistle and banjo. I figured if I was going to do music I might as well try and accomplish something. No point in just being shite at guitar.'

He says this with a laugh, but the point is that the water and surfing were the one constant through these shape-shifting years when he was, like most people in their early twenties, trying to figure things out. The diligent side of him – the teenager who left his chemistry books dog-eared and scored an impressive Leaving Certificate that promised him a smooth path into the professional life – still sometimes whispers in his ear. 'If I didn't surf I'd be pretty well taken care of by science right now,' he volunteers.

But that 'if' is bigger than Ben Bulben: it is impossible for McGoldrick to imagine his world without surfing. It fires his imagination and he talks about it in long, torrential, enthusiastic bursts while never losing sight of the fact that it has kind of taken ownership of him. 'That was the whole theme throughout the last eight years of my life. Since I was eighteen, surfing slowly took over and affected relationships, family and myself as a person. All I wanted to do was go surfing. I think Fergal is lucky with the break he got but he is also a really brave kid. The life of weekend surfing would not have worked for me. I wasn't that kind of a surfer. The first time I went to Clare was when I figured that out. The waves here at weekends are great. But to be up in Dublin when I knew Aileen's was pumping was a kind of a torture. It is an agonizing feeling. The sea has always been that womb and that cradle. The sea gives you health and happiness and it gave me a genuine spirituality too. I used to skateboard past the church every Sunday morning. I am quite a pious person but I felt I had my own Church.'

McGoldrick had come to the same realization as Kevin Naughton in California decades earlier. When he went surfing in Strandhill on those sleepy Sunday mornings when half the parish was at Mass and the other half in bed, he had virtual ownership of the sea. A few years ago he met a group of visiting Californian surfers out on the water and they were taken aback by how easy-going the Irish approach was. 'In California, nobody says zip. This is a bit of a fallen world anyhow in terms of society so places like Strandhill and Bundoran feel like the last bastion for surfing as it was years ago, where there is a kind of respect for other people. That's why you would hate to see the Irish tradition of surfing succumbing to corporatism and all that stuff.'

In the summer of his first year at Trinity, McGoldrick started visiting Clare regularly. He had been working on a building site in Sligo and jumped on a bus on Friday afternoon. He had heard of the local wave christened Bumbaloids by the gang of bodyboarders who pioneered it. He had everything packed – fins, wetsuit, wax, board. By the time he reached Charlestown he realized he had forgotten his contact lenses, without which he wouldn't spot a tsunami let alone a surf-worthy wave. After a night in a hostel with friends he had arranged to meet they headed towards Spanish Point and saw an impressive, angry break and guessed that must be the famous wave. They tried to paddle out, ignoring people on the coastline waving them in as if they were madmen. 'It was just this crazy wave breaking off Spanish Point,' he laughs. 'I took off on a couple and got the hell out of there.' It wasn't until they met Dan Skajarowski and Jack Johns that they found what they were looking for. The Cornish boys were sixteen years old and had been living in a tent and surfing all day long. 'I think they'd been surviving on baked beans for sixteen straight days,' McGoldrick marvels.

Skajarowski led the Sligo lads out for their first session at Bumbaloids, and as the day unfolded McGoldrick realized it would be one of the rare ones that you carry with you. The wave was everything he had imagined – wonderful and threatening and frightening. They came rolling in with a school of dolphins and the boys swam beneath the surface and watched them scooting about them, close enough to touch their skin. McGoldrick resists the hippy ethos associated with surfing, but there was no point in pretending that this wasn't a sublime moment. That was it for him and Clare. He rang his foreman and told him he was sick and surfed for another three days. He rang again and told him he still wasn't better and the foreman advised him to get better by Monday if he still wanted his job. After that, he was a regular visitor to Clare.

He can't remember when he first met Mickey Smith but he knew him from a magazine cover that had left him dumbstruck when he walked into a Sligo newsagent's and saw it sitting there alongside the fashion publications. Smith was bodyboarding in a dazzling emerald barrel and the banner headline proclaimed: 'This Is England'. But by the time McGoldrick met him, Smith was well into his fascination with Clare. He had already discovered Aileen's, and McGoldrick happened to be in Clare in the autumn week when Smith returned, intent on surfing it.

McGoldrick is courageous but he calls his own shots, and he elected to leave Aileen's on that first day. He returned a few weeks later, having absorbed what the others said about the wave and having taken sufficient time to think about whether he was ready to try it for himself. 'I have this thing when I get nervous where I hyperventilate,' he says of his first session at Aileen's. 'That was happening walking down the goats' trail. Your heart is in your mouth. It is a cliché, but still, when you paddle out there you have this reaction: I could really die here. It is a perfect wave but there is that gamble. It is a mixture of beauty and fear so when you are out there you tell yourself that if you are going for a small one, you might as well go for a good big one.'

He goaded himself along, picking off a few smaller waves and coming through unscathed and then feeling more confident and lucky as he paddled into bigger sets. He was delighted with the session, and then Smith suggested in that casual, easy-going way of his that he should head to Riley's that afternoon, that he was ready for it. McGoldrick had imagined Riley's as something similar to Aileen's: another terrific wave breaking well back from the coastline. But when he saw the way it reared and snapped so close to the rocky platform, he decided to pass. 'It took me another eight months to be ready to surf it. I backed out because Mickey was doing some pretty crazy stuff at that stage. It takes time. Like, last winter, I broke down so many barriers that I am getting pretty excited about the winter ahead.'

Over the years people kept coming to Clare, sometimes clutching Mickey Smith's phone number, and in the late winter of 2007 it was Tom Lowe's turn. He was rambling around with two of his oldest friends from St Ives, Matt Smith and Tom Greenway, in an Opel Kadett, looking for somewhere new to surf. He had first seen Smith playing in punk bands in summer bars around Cornwall when they were both little more than children. When he got to Clare he was awkward about calling him, going so far as to formally introduce himself when Smith picked up.

'Yeah, course I know who you are, Tom,' Smith laughed. 'What are you on about?'

Over five years later, sitting in Smith's house, Lowe could

admit the phone call changed his life. It was around Easter, and Lowe was recuperating from the latest of an impressive sequence of injuries: a broken foot he had just suffered at Riley's. He lives in Lanzarote now but travels to Shannon whenever the weather charts indicate a swell. He is on nodding terms with some of the staff at Shannon airport, who are used to seeing this tall, blond, perpetually cheerful Englishman lugging a surfboard through arrivals on evenings when the terminal is all but deserted.

Lowe grew up in St Ives and bounced between the localized surf influences and the mainstream English sports of rugby and football. He has the athletic cut of a rugby fullback and cricket was his best game but all he wanted to do was surf and skate. He ran about with a group trying their best to do what they believed skateboarders should do, flinging water bombs and eggs at police cars and making videos of their antics. His dad is Liverpudlian and his mum is from Tavistock, and he was just five when they split up. 'Wasn't the smoothest run at that age but it wasn't the hardest either because they get on so well now that you couldn't wish for anything more.' But childhood arrangements meant that he spent part of his time living with his father in the centre of St Ives and the rest of the time with his mother.

His father is classically Liverpudlian, believing there is nowhere like his home city, championing Everton FC and never allowing anything to faze him. 'You know the Scouser way?' Lowe asks, breaking into a perfect accent. 'Sound, mate. No biggie. He was always great in a crisis that way. So with Dad it was fish and chips, sausage and chips. With Mum it was pure health and organic . . . She is just super chilled about everything.' So he grew up seeing all aspects of Cornwall, from the quaint artisan shops to the full-on energy of St Ives in summer, listening to old-school 1970s surf men, hanging out in local bars where promising local bands violent with energy and ambition bloomed and died overnight, going to school and playing cricket, and becoming increasingly aware, because the streets of St Ives bustled with summer visitors and then fell quiet in winter, that there was Cornwall and then there was this other land out there called England that none of them quite knew.

Lowe happened to be one of those kids who was unable to help being good at sport and when he was eleven years old he was picked for the West of England schoolboys' cricket team. He remained an automatic choice for the next five years. And it was a big deal: tours to the West Indies and to South Africa, and rubbing shoulders with public school boys with cut-glass accents who, it turned out, were dead sound and often just as doubtful as he was about the whole scene. Lowe will always remember the coach's instruction before one match against the South Africans. 'Lowe, you are going to open. Big game. We need you.' And he hated it, hated this venomous ball spinning at his head, but even though one part of his mind was screaming at him to duck out of the way he had this reputation for stepping into it and making contact. He knew that it was a tremendous honour and that his parents were proud as punch but whenever he went to the nets to practise, it was out of duty. His mind was always drawn to the water; on his bedroom wall were surfing posters rather than mugshots of Mike Atherton. 'I just didn't enjoy it. I couldn't figure my game out. And, you know, I didn't even really know who I was at that point. But cricket was finished for me by the time I was sixteen. I knew then I just wanted to surf.'

When he left school he worked as a labourer in the summer and then began taking off in the winter for the fabulous places he had read about in magazines. Five years flew like that, and then one year he decided to go to Ireland instead.

Lowe was serious about surfing but had never once entered a competition or considered making a life out of it. Then, after that phone call, Mickey Smith took him to surf at Bumbaloids. 'These heavy waves just blew my mind. Mickey took pictures and I felt awkward as anything but he was just incredibly positive. He kept telling me to go for it . . . Nobody had ever spoken to me like that in the water before. Then we went round to his house and he showed me all these photographs and he told me that if I wanted, I could give this thing a go. Head to Australia, get some heavy waves, get a portfolio of pictures, get sponsorship; actually surf for a living. He practically wrote novels for me on my website in the beginning. It was Mickey who pushed me to take it seriously and to believe in myself.'

Dan Skajarowski took the plunge in 2007. He was to-ing and fro-ing so often that it became simpler just to relocate to Clare, where he has been ever since, working in a restaurant in Lahinch and giving surf lessons in the summer. His older brother Steph followed him early in 2008. 'I was always over visiting Mickey when I could,' Steph said one sleepy March morning in Joe's, a café/institution just off the Lahinch promenade. 'Ryanair wasn't the cheapest thing. And this place felt very like home anyway: it is the west country and it is tourist dependent. You have these mad summers and then the winters are a whole other story . . . You know, what's beautiful about the place could also drive you mad.'

Steph witnessed the country slowing down shortly after his arrival. On all of his previous visits to Mickey he couldn't help but be aware of the purpose with which Irish people seemed to move, of expensive cars glimmering in the sunshine, of the eye-popping prices of takeaway coffee, of how everyone seemed pleased with life if slightly manic. 'You could tell that things were good. People were spending and people were happy. And then literally over the next twelve months everything started to dry up. You could see it here. Staff numbers were cut and hours were cut and there wasn't any sense of money out there. People had been throwing money around for a lot of years and all of a sudden they were in survival mode. That is how it has been since.'

Steph delivers this summary cheerfully, but then he grew up with seasonality in St Just. The summers in Lahinch are still relatively busy and he gets regular hours during the winter as well, when he can surf more. He likes being close at hand to watch his brother. 'I remember the first time I took Dan and Pirin [Dan's twin brother] out. It was a sunny day, waves chest high, perfect. I stuck a pair of flippers on them and paddled them out to a bank just off shore, and, bless them, they were terrified. The irony is that I will go to the cliffs now and watch what Dan is doing there and I will be terrified.'

Before Steph moved to Clare he had often heard Mickey speak in glowing terms of a young Mayo lad he had happened upon in Mullaghmore. 'Fergal may still have been in school then. Yeah, Mickey was raving about this young lad with a great attitude and talent. After I moved here Fergal was coming down the whole time and he was about to break through. Now, every time I watch him and Tom I see them doing things that haven't been done before.'

Lowe can't even recall how he first met Fergal Smith. It may have been on the roadside on the way to some wave or other, or in the water at Aileen's. In the beginning, Lowe was a bit taken aback by the blazing independence this Irish youngster displayed. The first time they surfed at Aileen's, Smith announced that he was going to paddle over to the nearby Lauren's wave and promptly did so. He had no company and there was nobody to help him if things went wrong. 'I thought he was mental, to be honest,' Lowe says. 'He was away for an hour. I was there thinking: well, he's a bit different.'

It was around then that Mickey Smith, on another solitary ramble along the coastline, not far from the opulent Doonbeg golf resort, stumbled on another gem of a wave. Unlike Aileen's, this one was completely obscured from view and was farcically difficult to get to. Smith loved it. This was the wave he would, in time, name after Riley, his nephew in Cornwall.

By coincidence, Smith was due to photograph the Australian big wave surfer Paul Morgan in Clare that week along with Pierre Louis-Costes, a French teenager who would become the leading bodyboarder in the world. He wanted the visitors to see the wave straight away. He asked Tom Lowe to guide them to the wave. And so it was that Morgan, just hours after a gruelling flight from Australia, found himself tramping along a muddy field on the outskirts of Clare with an Englishman he didn't know. Mickey Smith scooted across from Doonbeg pier on the one jet-ski they possessed at that time. Lowe had never towed into a wave before and he was petrified: nobody had ever surfed at Riley's before, he was in awe of Morgan, and technically he just wasn't sure how to go about towing in. 'It was straight in at the deep end. I ended up just grabbing the rope and crawling on to my knees and elbows, and by the time I stood up I was on the bloody wave. It was a good solid six-foot wave and then I was in the barrel and out again and it was one of the best waves of my life at that point.'

For a few weeks after that Riley's remained a glittering secret, a brilliantly promising wave that was confrontational in its beauty and its power. Nothing about the way it broke disguised the fact that you could get hurt there, and over the months and years that followed, they all did. One day at Tom Doidge-Harrison's surf shed, a group of men called in to discuss boards he was shaping for them. After they left, Tom pointed at one and said, 'That's Peter Conroy. He broke his back at Riley's.' The one blessing was that Conroy works as a paramedic and had the composure to talk his companions through the ordeal of carefully lifting him on to the back of a jet-ski and back to land where he was transported to hospital. Conroy made a full recovery and returned to surfing, but he stands as proof of just how treacherous the wave can be. Others would suffer similar mishaps.

Every so often, Fergal or Mickey or the Skajarowskis will call up to Tom Doidge-Harrison to discuss making a new board. He might not have seen them for a few months and then a swell gifts itself and he is out on the water with them for hours every day. Harrison is clearly besotted with board-shaping and it is a demanding art. Even on damp days the air in the shed feels terribly brittle and dry. He spends hours masked up and working in the whine of the planer and the dust, often until ten and eleven in the evening.

'It is knackering,' he admitted one day, stepping outside his shed into the damp afternoon. He couldn't have been more dust-covered had he spent a working shift down in the mines he visits. 'It is really physical. It is hard on your joints. The materials are carcinogenic. It is dirty. Messy, loud. It is like a job but it is not nine to five. I can go in and hang out with Raquel and Nora for a few hours and then come out in the evening. I do love surfboards. That is what it comes down to. They are amazing. And I am careful about it. These boards have my initials on them so I'd feel bad if there was something poor out there.'

Surfers often call up to him with a vague notion of a board they think would be ideal for a particular wave. Sometimes they come in with very definite specifications, or they want him to come up with ideas. The process is always the same. It begins with the paring down of a foam blank to the agreed dimensions of length and width, taking care that the rail – the sculpted perimeter of the board which defines its speed and mobility – is precisely as outlined. Then Harrison takes the board into a back room where rolls of fibreglass hang against the wall and he lays a strip out on the foam board twice and trims it, placing two layers on top of the board and one on the bottom and afterwards sealing them with resin. Fins and a leash plug are attached, and then he sands the board again to achieve the desired shape. It is both heavy-duty and painstakingly precise, and it is hardly mass production: Harrison gets through about two boards during a working week uninterrupted by surfing. In a small factory with just four shapers, they might produce four boards a day.

Sometimes he hears of a board that left his studio only a day earlier getting smashed to bits after just hours in the water. Once, Fergal Smith collected a board from him, headed straight out with it and got caught side-paddling into a heavy winter wave which just broke it like it was a twig. Smith had already paid for the board but he was almost apologetic because he knew the time and craft that had gone into making it. 'It's disappointing when that happens,' Harrison says, 'but you just have to accept that it's part of it. And to be honest, having the likes of Fergal and Mickey using my boards feels like a validation of their quality.'

Bill Keane was in New York when he realized that surfing had elbowed its way into a different league of commercial muscle. He was happily wandering through Times Square enjoying the insane neon of the place when he saw that two of the biggest retail shop fronts were selling surf wear. He found himself completely and inexplicably dismayed. It seemed like the final irrefutable proof that surfing had shaken off the last of its countercultural traditions to become just another leisure industry.

'I just said, "Fuck this," and turned on my heels,' he laughs.

It is a common reaction: surfing devotees are always fretting about its soul, and while they do so others make millions selling designer T-shirts. But Keane is no sentimentalist. He makes no secret of his admiration for the coming generation. A few years ago he was in Hawaii watching the local crowd surfing Pipeline, the fabled North Shore left-breaking wave which, because of its popularity and force, has earned a reputation for being the most dangerous break in the world. Keane was both

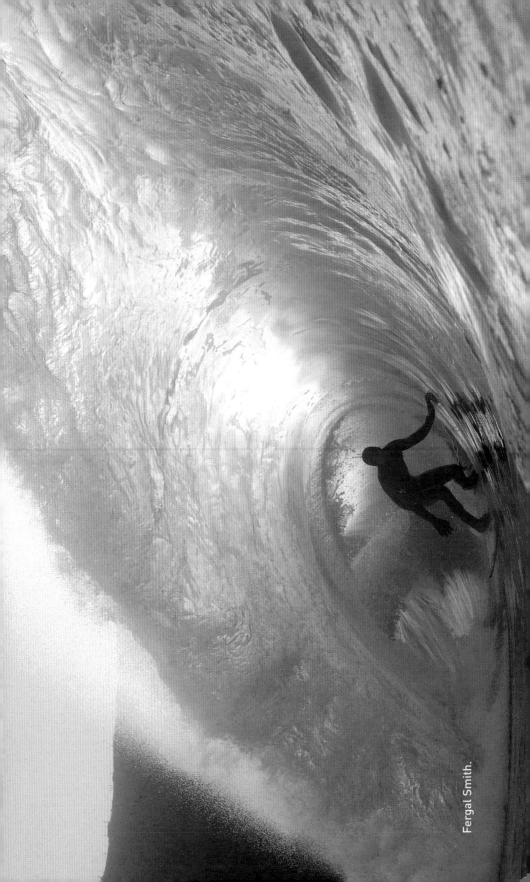

Fergal Smith.

Fergal Smith.

Above left: Fergal Smith and (**right**) Mickey Smith.

Below: Mickey on the cliffs.

Above left: Mickey Smith with his sister Cherry at the Reading Festival, and (**right**) Cherry's son Riley, after whom the wave was named.

Below: John McCarthy.

Dan Skajarowski.

Steph Skajarowski, Dan's brother.

Tom Doidge-Harrison with his daughter Nora.

Above: Dave Blount.

Right: Tom Lowe.

repelled and fascinated by the crowds and the aggression of the place, and was there strictly as a spectator. 'Throw me in with the bulls at Pamplona any day of the week,' he says. 'Place is carnage: the last place I'd ever want to surf. It is vicious and the crowd ten times more vicious.'

Keane noted the etiquette on the water. He saw a body-boarder dropping in on a surfer, forcing him to abandon his wave. The surfer gestured at the culprit but that was it. What got Keane, though, was that when the surfer eventually came in, his friends were waiting to berate him. 'They wanted to know why he hadn't beaten the shit out of the bodyboarder.' The atmosphere was heavily territorial and localized. Keane got talking with a French surfer who had shown up for seven years on the trot before he was accepted by the local posse.

One day, Keane was sitting on the beach watching the ritual play itself out in the waves when a lifeguard came running up to him.

'Are you Bill? We got your buddy.'

Keane was travelling alone so he was mystified. When he reached the lifeguard's hut there was a familiar face lying on a spinal board with a collar around his neck.

'Hiya, Fergal,' Bill said, grinning down at the Mayo man. 'How are you?'

'Grand, Bill,' Smith replied. 'Not a bother.'

For Keane, the moment was the most wonderfully illuminating proof of how far Irish surfing had come since he first launched himself into the waves in the 1980s.

Part of him can't help but pine a little for the lost sense that surfing was something mysterious. Now there is information and films and photographs from all over the world. Everything is seen instantly. He finally met his hero, Wayne Lynch – the other surfer in the film he watched on that rainy Saturday years earlier – when the Australian was walking out of a pub in Bundoran as Keane was walking in. They had a brief, pleasant chat. It was further confirmation that even though its tentacles reach the more remote coastlines of the planet, the surfing community is fairly small and always in flux. That is why the sense of an era passing is unique to every generation.

'Fergal always says the best time is now,' Keane says. 'And for him, that's definitely true.'

It seems as if every single person who ever committed themselves to surfing feels an instinctive urge to preserve things just as they are. It is impossible. Seamus McGoldrick's way of keeping the mystery of what he does alive runs counter-intuitive to his interest in science. 'I don't much care about the mechanics of the wave. I understand it a bit but physics is quite flimsy anyway. But I surf: why should I understand it? I just want to read waves. After that, well, water weighs a cubic tonne per metre so you can imagine how many tonnes are contained in those waves. That is why limbs get broken or leashes snapped. But it is too chaotic to understand. It is a mystic thing. You can be as logical as you want but when you talk about the wind and waves and the ocean, these elemental things go beyond that.'

Maybe what they have in Clare is going to change and therefore be lost too. Since Tom Doidge-Harrison started surfing in the county he has seen a new generation of young surfers coming through. The water is getting crowded. 'The thing is, I am part of that change. Things are always going to change so you might as well roll with it. I can't have too strong an opinion because I altered things myself by moving here.'

Sometimes he worries that someone young and promising will get caught out by not paying enough respect. He has seen surfboards fall off the back of jet-skis, people circling back to look for them, but the thing has vanished. 'A big white thing that floats! And they just disappear. So if someone went missing between Doolin and the cliffs, you might never be heard of [again]. Surfing the waves: what Fergal and Mickey and Tom do when they are surfing those big hollow waves that break into shallow water, that is physically quite dangerous. Big waves that rumble and can hold you under water for thirty seconds are dangerous. But the thing that could catch you is getting walloped on the head by your own board on a smallish day and getting knocked unconscious. What is dangerous, I think, is when people aren't aware where the danger lies.'

But there are still days when they have Aileen's all to themselves. The best part for Harrison is when he paddles out and meets one of the others, someone he may not have seen for weeks or months. 'There is no gallery. There is no stadium. It makes a difference when your friends are out there for sure. It's like . . . playing.'

4

Winter Days

On New Year's Day, Fergal Smith woke up in Cornwall. The last day of 2011 had ebbed away pleasantly and on dry land. He was staying with his girlfriend Tess's family and they had all spent the afternoon mucking around with Riley and Kalle, Mickey's nephews. Although Fergal has prodigious energy levels, he discovered that children have the power to do what the ocean hasn't yet achieved: they leave him knackered. 'They're incredible,' he recalled, shaking his head as though he had finally met his match for pure adrenalin. 'You could be out playing for three, four hours and you think that's it, they are going to need a rest. But they just keep on going.'

That night they did a tour of the pubs in St Ives. Fergal was happy to act as chauffeur for the gang because he knew he had an early start the following morning. The itch was back. He had been browsing the weather charts over the previous few days and noticed that the conditions looked promising for a particular break off the west coast of Ireland. He knew that the journey would probably be more trouble than it was worth. But the break is infrequent and he couldn't bear the thought of missing it. And so began the usual dash of changing flights and checking ferry times and packing bags at the last minute. 'Tess is used to me at this stage,' he smiles. He said his goodbyes early, drove up to Bristol airport, got on a flight to Dublin, took a bus across Ireland and made the last ferry out to the island that evening. His brother Kevin and Darragh, his friend from home, had booked into a hostel on New Year's Eve and they were waiting for him when he arrived. They made flasks of ginger tea and cooked some rice and peppers, packed their gear and set the alarm clocks for seven in the morning.

The second day of January was wickedly cold, and because the schools and businesses were still out for the seasonal holidays the roads were deserted. At half past eight in the morning it was three degrees Celsius and half dark and no Christmas tree was lit. There was no news on the radio, just chart hits and a documentary about Stephen Hunt, the Wolverhampton Wanderers and Ireland football player. He chatted happily about his football life to the backdrop of cheering crowds and sounded very far removed from the barren road out to the ferry port. The sea was choppy even at the port. Tourists began showing up for the morning sailing in ones and twos: American students, honeymooner types, a group of stoical Scandinavians and one or two islanders heading back from the mainland. People were half perished just from walking from the ticket office to the boat and the coffee vendor was doing brisk business. 'Are you sure?' he asked someone as the ferry began to reverse out of its dock. 'Because it's going to be rough in a few minutes and I've no lids.'

He wasn't joking. Soon the ferry was punching through heavy, lazy breakers that caused it to lurch and list. Laughter gave way to green faces and passengers began ducking their heads into plastic bags while others stumbled drunkenly for the deck, gripping the railing of the boat and directing their gaze into the sharp morning wind. The sea was a dazzling opal. The ferrymen gathered around the coffee kiosk and they moved as if they could have danced the foxtrot on the swaying boat. Most passengers were queasy but they were pleased too because the wildness of the journey gave the trip a stamp of authenticity: it enhanced the sense that they really were heading towards the remotest edge of Europe and that they were, at last, closing in on the real Ireland, land of knitwear, piseogs and traditional music. Still, tour guides were loitering at the pier when the ferry docked, promising to spare the visitors the spitting rain and lonely wind by giving them a seat in a heated, comfortable bus. Some accepted; others made for the pubs.

They all missed what would have been the most exotic and unlikely sight of all.

Fergal Smith was already out on the water but he was secluded from view and finding him involved a barren walk away along the coast road where there was no sound except the sea and a dog howling from behind a gate in one of the cottages. The day couldn't decide what it wanted to be: rain spat with enthusiasm for about fifteen seconds and then a bright winter sun came out again. It didn't seem likely that there was anyone out on the water but then, after about a twenty-minute walk, a shadow moved across the face of a wave which seemed to break at a weird side angle on a corner of the island, hammering into a rocky promontory rather than running its natural course into the shore. The wave died and the water calmed for a few seconds and again this long black shadow moved across the brilliant emerald of the Atlantic. And there he was.

The boys were dressed for the elements. Kevin was wrapped up in yellow oilskins and hunkered down beneath a stone wall, his camera fixed on the wave. Darragh was already standing in his wetsuit, firing intense looks at the surf and convincing himself that he wanted to go in. The only other person there was Declan, a Dublin surfing enthusiast who has been living on the island for over a decade. 'I wouldn't claim to be local,' he clarified. 'I know a family who moved here in the 1800s who aren't seen as local.' He knew of Fergal through reading surf magazines and then happened to bump into him one time on the island.

We stood watching Fergal surf the most westerly wave in Europe, hunkering down behind a stone wall whenever brief, intense bursts of rain passed through. Behind us, stone walls crisscrossed the fields and there were a few ruined cottages here and there. This was Synge's fabled country, where the sea was a source of livelihood and superstition and death. There is a passage in Synge's book *The Aran Islands* that chronicles the difficulty the islanders had in navigating the waves on rough days:

> In bad weather four men will often stand for nearly an hour at the top of the slip with a curragh in their hands, watching a point of rock towards the south where they can see the strength of the waves that are coming in.

The instant a break is seen they swoop down to the surf, launch their curragh and pull out to sea with incredible speed. Coming to land is attended with the same difficulty, and if their moment is badly chosen they are likely to be washed sideways and swamped among the rocks.

This continual danger, which can only be escaped by extraordinary personal dexterity, has had considerable influence on the local character, as the waves have made it impossible for clumsy, foolhardy or timid men to live on these islands.

What would old JM have made of Fergal Smith if he could have seen him on this island? Even a century after Synge was tramping around the islands with his notebook there is something terrifically maverick about the sight of this slender figure in a black water suit with green surfboard, climbing over the rearing waves and waiting and watching.

The sets broke frequently and noisily but he had to leave most of them be. Later he would explain that they were just too unreliable – they either wouldn't let him in or he knew that the drop was going to be too steep for him to make. Smith simply isn't interested in waves he knows he can't make: it's a waste of energy. He waited for forty minutes before he even attempted to ride a wave. In all, he was in the water for five hours and he surfed about two waves that he was happy with. Most of the time he spent just fighting the constant rolling surf simply to stay in the right spot. The sets were unpredictable, and every so often snarling, curling monstrosities would rise out of nothing and crash with an impressive percussive thunderclap. 'Beasties,' Declan said with a grin whenever they appeared. They were backlit, and the sunshine gave them a beatific quality. Behind them the ocean stretched emptily towards America.

After a while Darragh joined Fergal in the water and it seemed less lonesome with two people out there. Darragh got some decent waves and came to shore again after about an hour. Fergal had spent most of that time treading water and waiting. Kevin kept his camera trained on his brother the entire time. It was just too risky to pause record because after an hour of watching and waiting the wave that Fergal had been waiting for could arrive in a second. And that was how it happened here. One second he was lying on his board paddling, looking behind and gauging a breaking wave, and the next he was poised, crouched on the lip of the wave as it rose, and then falling through air for a split second as he dropped down into the face of the wave.

If you slow down the footage Kevin took you can see Fergal's silhouette on the board, perfectly balanced and in control, and then almost straight away a perfect veil of water just sweeps over him in an arc and he disappears. He glides through the liquid cavern even as it forms around him. Modern photographic technology has elevated surfing stills into the realms of art, but nothing compares to the fleeting splendour of someone gliding through the heart of a wave before your eyes. The wall of the wave would thin out in places so that we could see a ghostly version of him passing through it for a split second, then the water would cascade so thickly that he vanished entirely, and just when you presumed that it had collapsed in on him, he appeared again. Then the barrel fell away and Fergal glided up the face of the wave and back down.

'Pretty cool, that carve section at the end,' he would say later when reviewing the film Kevin had taken. 'It's like a little skate ramp.'

All of that took less than ten seconds – though it seems longer even just to watch somebody surfing a wave like that – and Fergal stayed out for another ninety minutes without experiencing anything as satisfactory. Kevin could tell that he was exhausted by then. It was about three in the afternoon and the waves were turning choppy and broken but he knew his brother was caught in that place of knowing he was nearly spent but desperately wanting to stay out for just one more, and just one more, and just one more. Eventually, after surfing a wave that disintegrated into broken foam even as he committed to it, he paddled to shore and carried his board over the big smooth rocks. He moved lightly on his feet but when he came closer he looked destroyed. His lips were bluish and his eyes were bright, like someone with a fever. He said that his head was sore and buzzing, and because he was still wearing his hood he was shouting a little. Kevin handed him some ginger tea and he cradled the flask cup in his hands, moving his feet to stay warm while talking about the session. He'd put on a waterproof jacket and was talking away but he looked hypothermic. He had only a vague idea if the waves he had surfed had been good and he was half thinking of going back out. 'Just to bring the six foot three out and do a few turns. But I dunno if the body is in it,' he laughed. 'The brain wants to do it but the body's fucken broken.' He changed back into his clothes with the speed of movement you would expect of anyone who has to strip out of a soaked wetsuit on a damp laneway on the edge of Ireland in early January. Then he ate the rice and pepper concoction he and Darragh had prepared the night before and some chocolate he had been given by his hosts in Cornwall. Within minutes he seemed heated up and fully recovered again.

Declan had brought his car down to help them to transport the wetsuits and boards back to the hostel. Over tea they looked at the film Kevin had taken and it was then, with the wind no longer howling in his ears, that Fergal could begin to assess what he had been doing all day. The boys watched the waves he had ridden on a laptop in the kitchen. Outside, the lights had come on at the pier and the day-trippers were assembling for the ferry ride back to the mainland. The boys were staying for the evening, though, and would reward themselves with a night in the pub.

They surfed all the next day, and then Fergal returned to Clare. That weekend he and Tess went to a party at a friend's house in Kerry and he forgot his jacket and got caught in a shower. It was through that, not the hours he spent in the Atlantic, that he caught a flu which floored him for a week.

The days roll into one another, and that is how the seasons define themselves. When there are no waves Fergal spends his days running, swimming, maintaining the jet-ski, catching up with correspondence, working on his website, working on the vegetable plot he has planned for the back garden – 'Just in case it all comes crashing down' – and keeping in touch with Adam Warren and his other sponsors. There are mellow days when Clare folds in on itself and you can't even take a short trip to the shops without getting soaked. But those days are fine. He needs them.

He spent most of the winter trying to convince Adam that he didn't need to be in Hawaii to make a surf film with the others. His idea was to devote his time to Irish waters and have Mickey shoot and edit the months of footage they took and to add that to the final film. Surfing winter waves in Ireland was what attracted Analog to him in the first place so he didn't see the point in appearing in a film featuring azure waters and tropical sunshine. But the possibility of going to Hawaii was there in the background for a few months. In the meantime he just kept his head down, living and working and watching the weather charts.

Less than two weeks after his first surf of the year, Aileen's broke in earnest. It was a bitingly cold Sunday afternoon but even so a long line of cars was parked haphazardly on the narrow road at the cliff top, some festooned with surf logos and with boards tied to roof racks. A small crowd of spectators had gathered at the cliff's edge to watch the wave. Far below, fifteen surfers were out there. They looked impossibly small and insignificant from the vantage point of the cliff.

Fergal's day had started early: he made sure he was at Riley's before eight o'clock to get the best of the morning tide. But the sky was blue–black when they arrived and they had to sit in the car until there was enough light just to see where they were going. Smith still had a horrible cold and the neck injury he had suffered the previous summer had flared. Nothing about that morning was inviting. 'The hardest thing is waiting in the water. You go in two hours before high tide and you surf for three hours and you've hit the bottom ten times and you are wrecked. There is still an hour of tide left and everything is telling you to leave but you can't because there might be that one amazing wave in the next hour. What you are doing at that point isn't even surfing. You are just sitting on the board and your core body temperature goes down and that's the most draining thing of all. But you need to be ready to go and feel full of energy that you don't have at that point. That is the big mental pressure. Most people want to get out because it is a horrendous feeling. You are shivering and the very last thing you want to do is take off on a heavy wave.'

After leaving Riley's he swallowed some soup he had in a flask and took off for Aileen's, going through the tedium of changing out of his wetsuit to make the drive over from Doonbeg to the Cliffs of Moher and then pulling it back on again. He was taken aback by how busy the water was that afternoon but was delighted to see one particular face in the crowd. 'Cain Kilcullen. Yeah. He had never been out here and he's an amazing surfer so it was about time. He should have been surfing Aileen's for years.'

Kilcullen is from Enniscrone in County Sligo and even as a teenager he seemed to surf with a white chocolate smoothness and effortlessness that distinguished him from the crowd. When Kevin Naughton first saw Kilcullen surfing he recognized instantly that everything about the style and imagination with which he expressed himself would turn heads in California. Kilcullen seemed like proof of a new breed in Ireland, a natural born surfer.

Kilcullen is the same age as Smith. They spent their formative years surfing together and have both won national championships. But Kilcullen is as easy-going in his approach as Smith is fiercely single-minded, and so it was that it had taken the Sligo man until January 2012 to finally head down to surf at Aileen's. He couldn't have picked a more crowded day. The waves were powerful and consistent but the line-up was disorganized; boards were flying everywhere and there were fewer waves surfed than on most other days. As ever, Smith was a bit stressed by the messiness of the afternoon, half concentrating on taking off on his own waves but always wondering if someone was about to get seriously hurt. But he had a perfect view of Kilcullen's moment.

'This wave came in and it had a seriously good shape. I could have tried to catch it but I was a bit too far behind it, and Cain was perfectly placed. There is a little bit further out where you can catch bigger waves that roll you into the wave itself. That's where I was. Cain was waiting inside a bit. So this wave wasn't quite big enough to break outside but it broke perfectly for him. He just put his head down and I was shouting after him. I was stoked to see it.'

Kilcullen wore a red wetsuit and from the cliff top he looked incandescent against the dark green of the water and the milky sky. As always the crowd watched first to see if the surfer was about to get chewed up in the wave, but Kilcullen's drop down was so smooth and he read it so perfectly that a smattering of applause – like something on a village cricket green in Shropshire – had broken out even before he emerged from the barrel. Smith felt delighted just watching it: he had always known that Kilcullen could easily translate his talent into surfing bigger waves and now it was happening before his eyes. 'It was a really cleanly shaped barrel and he surfed it properly. That was what was great.'

Nestled on a promontory halfway down the cliff, Kevin Smith captured every second of Kilcullen's wave. When there is a swell at Aileen's, the goats' trail down to the foot of the cliffs becomes a temporary locker room. Bundles of clothes are stored behind rocks, and surfboards lie here and there. You can often find a few photographers sheltering against the rock face and Kevin takes up a position that is impossible to see from the cliff top, scrabbling across the near vertical bank of rough grass and across loose stones to take his place on a perch that is sheltered from the wind and holds a perfect view of the wave.

Not long after Kilcullen surfed that wonderful wave he took off again, but this time he learned just how capricious Aileen's can be: he was unceremoniously decked as the wave crumbled and then held under water for what Kevin Smith estimated to be over twenty seconds. The wave washed him towards the boulders underneath the cliff and when he finally got his breath back he discovered the water had also taken half his board as a memento. He had no choice but to go in and make the long climb up the trail. His face was red from the rawness of the day and from those long seconds under the water but his eyes were shining: as debuts at Aileen's go, Kilcullen couldn't have expected anything more spectacular.

Soon after that the others began to paddle for home in ones and twos. Kevin had been hoping that the late afternoon sky would blossom into one of the winter-red sunsets he had begun to photograph, but instead everything turned shadowy and cold. He packed up his gear and scrambled across the scrub grass to where Fergal had left his bag on the trail. Those of us standing about halfway up could see Fergal paddling in with Hugo Galloway and Tom Gillespie. Because the boulders around them were so big and the light was fading, they looked elfin in size. After climbing up the trail Fergal was numb with tiredness but in terrific form. 'I was at the stage when I felt like I just couldn't get a wave. But it was a good day overall. This is just the halfway point of the season so hopefully there will be some good days to come.'

That night he phoned Cain Kilcullen just to talk about the afternoon. By then the evening news bulletins on the radio and television were carrying the grim news that a fishing trawler had sunk near the mouth of Glandore harbour in Cork and that five men were missing. It was hard to believe that those same turbulent waters which had given them all such pleasure that afternoon was also the source of unimaginable sadness an hour or two further down the coast.

5

No Man's Land

It's not as if they ever forget to respect the sea. Sometimes surfing can seem like the most frivolous pursuit in the world. It is, after all, about nothing more than chasing an intensely personal wish for escapism, about spending hour after hour in the water for a few seconds of transcendent experience. Surfers can earn their living on the water but it is not like fishing: it is not essential. Surfing is a life choice or a vocation more than a livelihood. And surfers are willing to put themselves in dangerous places just to chase that.

One of the paradoxes of surfing is that for all the death-defying wipe-outs and the tales of braggadocio that accompany them, relatively few surfers actually drown. In 1992 a strange and wonderful essay entitled 'Playing Doc's Games' appeared in the *New Yorker* magazine. It was seven years in the composition, ran to some 40,000 words and dealt with the enduring obsession of the author, William Finnegan, with surfing. In particular it chronicled a period he spent surfing the hostile, challenging waters around the bay area of San Francisco in the company of Mark Renneker, a force of nature who somehow balances a working life as a doctor specializing in family practice and cancer research with his passion for seeking out remote, extreme waves. Renneker also found time to establish the Surfer's Medical Association and is a reliable voice on the instances of fatalities in the sport.

In Matt Warshaw's endlessly fascinating *Encyclopaedia of Surfing*, Renneker is quoted from a piece he wrote following the 1994 drowning of Hawaiian big wave surfer Mark Foo: 'Deaths from surfing are so rare that each one becomes newsworthy.' Renneker estimated that the death rate from surfing is 1 in 100,000 – lower than in skateboarding or snow sports. Foo's death at Mavericks was given the international treatment not only because he was one of the most marketable names in surfing but because the wave that claimed him was relatively small: unquestionably dangerous at twenty feet, but Foo had made his name by tearing into a thirty-foot wave at Waimea and coming out unscathed. That December visit to Mavericks was his first, and his presence there, alongside fellow Hawaiian legend Ken Bradshaw, was regarded as an event: it was as if the Hawaiians were giving the wave their benediction by travelling there to surf it. Foo's last wave was captured on grainy film, and although it was studied in freeze frame a thousand times, the precise cause of his death was never determined. Maybe his leash became entangled in rocks on the ocean floor, or maybe he received a concussive blow from a board passing overhead as he tried to resurface. Whatever happened, he drowned. A week later, in a much-publicized ceremony held at Mavericks, Foo's ashes were scattered in the water.

Just like the gods of the rock music world who flame out early, a strange sort of immortality is conferred on dead surfers. Every decade has its totemic death. Like that of poor Dickie Cross from Honolulu, just seventeen on the December day in 1943 when he was cut off from the mainland by huge, impassable waves that broke relentlessly and who in a desperate bid to make it back to the shore at Waimea lost his board, disappeared in a churning set of waves and was never found. His death resonated so strongly that a decade passed before surfers went back to Waimea. Or that of Eddie Aikau, another Honolulu lad who had won admiration and acclaim for his eye-catching, original style and who in 1978 was one of fifteen crew members taking part in a 2,000-mile voyage on a replica Polynesian canoe they intended to sail from Hawaii to Tahiti. Halfway across the boat capsized. The crew was stranded, clinging to the wreck. Aikau took control, setting off on a ten-foot surfboard for an island over ten miles away. A rescue boat arrived to pick up the crew but Aikau was lost. An annual big-wave tournament is held in his name each year.

Of course ordinary, anonymous surfers suffer tragedy without any such acknowledgement from the sport. But even in this wider context death is rare. Pipeline may be regarded as the most lethal wave because of the crowds drawn to it, but the place averages one fatality every second season.

The lesson is not about how often surfers drown so much as absorbing the fact that it can happen. If someone as accomplished and confident as Mark Foo can go that way, anyone can, at any time. Some surfers, like Aikau and Foo, pass into legend through their deaths. Their names are sacred touch-stones for what can go wrong. Every local surf spot in the world has its own stories. Clare is no different.

One day Dan Skajarowski showed up at Riley's already wearing his wetsuit, carrying his bodyboard under his arm and skipping across the long stone shelf as if it were hot coals beneath his feet. The shelf is absurdly slippery even in mild weather and every surfer who has ever walked across it has invariably ended up on his arse. Eventually they figured out that the best thing to do was just skip across, never really gaining traction. Skajarowski made it look easy. When he got to the little mound of rock near where they like to paddle out to the wave, he put down his board and began a series of stretches. Most of the others were already in the water and it was a dazzling September afternoon, clean and sunny. He could hear the whoops coming from the water but he was in no rush. He had just driven from Sligo and his knee felt stiff – the legacy of a horrible injury he suffered two years earlier at Riley's.

It happened after a tumble that seemed to be identical to the hundreds he had experienced previously. He had been in the water for four hours and was feeling almost drowsy with happiness because the waves had just presented themselves perfectly for him. He was almost spent, so he waited for a smaller wave so he could see out the session with a bit of fun. His brother Steph had just left the water and was standing on the platform. Seamus McGoldrick had begun to make for home when Dan paddled into what would be his final wave. Just as the wave formed into a barrel he felt a wobble beneath his board, a sort of speed bump that threw him off balance.

He waited for the inevitable sensation of being spun up into the wave. Except that this time the water sent him spearing towards the bed of rocks submerged a few feet below the surface. There was a split second of surprise when his knee clattered into something hard and viciously sharp because the unspoken belief at Riley's was that you will get away with it if you know what you are doing. And Skajarowski always knew what he was doing. Then the most searing pain he had ever known went shooting through his body.

Just like that he was screaming, and just like that he was in shock. The waves kept arriving and battering him on the head anyway. He might as well have been a zookeeper who suddenly realizes the tiger is no longer playing with him but mauling him. Seamus McGoldrick paddled over to him within seconds. It occurred to Dan that Seamus was at once both the best and worst man in the world to come to his assistance in a moment like this. His unflappability was reassuring. But his idea – to help Skajarowski to remount his board and then help him towards the shore by giving him an encouraging little shove so he could paddle in on a smaller wave that came their way – was less successful.

For the next few minutes, as Dan tried to think his way through the screaming pain, he was reminded of the foolishness of what they were doing. People who have been given precise directions to Riley's often have difficulty locating the place. The cliff is such a sheer drop and the wave hugs the coastline so tightly that you have to be standing on the very edge just to see the surfers. It is completely secluded. Skajarowski knew he had done some serious damage to his knee (the kneecap would later prove to be shattered) and hadn't the faintest idea about how he was going to get back to civilization. He experienced a brief, terrifying vision of trying to hobble across the field with Steph and Seamus acting as a pair of crutches. Briars, brambles, ditches – he knew it would be impossible. Just getting out of the water promised to be an ordeal. And even if he managed that he faced a 500-metre walk across the rock platform before he even began to negotiate the fields and barbed-wire fences that separated them from their van. As it was, he just kept bobbing about in the shallows, each wave that crashed over him delivering an even more severe level of pain, as if to hammer home the perils of trying to have fun on this patch of coast.

Steph could hear Dan shouting 'Get me in, get me in' the entire time and the distress in his voice cannoned off the cliff drop. And Steph carried the oldest child's sense of responsibility: even though it wasn't his fault, it was his fault. Dan's face was white as flour by the time McGoldrick managed to fish him from the water and after the briefest consultation they made the phone call that all surfers dread, summoning the coastguard to come and fetch them. It was the ultimate admission that the wave had left them helpless.

'I remember kind of crapping myself because I wasn't in Ireland very long and I didn't know what the deal was,' Dan recalled on a scorching summer day in Lahinch, when the promenade was crowded and pop music drifted out from all the cafés. 'I wasn't even sure if anyone would come.' Dan works in a local restaurant in the summer and gives surf lessons, leaving him with little time to find waves himself during the tourist season. The Skajarowski surname is the result of a Polish man who made his way to England and, as his great-grandson laughs, 'found a Cornish wife and settled down'. Dan is tall and languidly athletic and has done his share of roaming also, but he visited Ireland with his parents when he was still in school and he remembers his initial jaunt with Jack Johns, when he bumped into Seamus McGoldrick and Tom Gillespie, as probably the most fun he's ever had. 'It seemed to bucket down for the entire time, much too wet to use the tents. But there was a small leak in the car. It was so small that we had to sleep upright in the seats. But it was great. We slept no problem.' It was also the most broke he has ever been.

When Skajarowski was growing up in Cornwall, his older brother Steph was friendly with Mickey Smith, who used to come over from Penzance. Dan's twin, Piran, took to the water and caught the surfing bug straight away. But Dan was more cautious in the beginning. He started bodyboarding because of convenience: their nearest beach is negotiable only by walking hundreds of stone-cut steps down the cliff face and it was easier to carry a light foam board than a full surfboard at that age. Steph pushed him to go further in the water, to be braver and more confident. But it took time. 'I remember the first time I ever surfed over rocks and crying my eyes out. The water was only waist high and it is one of the only reefs in Cornwall. I was just too scared. It was just the fact of the unknown. But it was around then that I realized that this is all I wanted to do.'

By the time he was a teenager he had the same impatience as the others to get through school and get moving, working an evening job through his college years until he had scraped together £5,000 so he could surf all the places he had seen and read about in the magazines: Bali, Tahiti, Mexico. In Puerto

Escondido he saw a surfer making the mistake of dropping in front of three or four locals. They followed him in when he left the water and then attacked him with baseball bats, leaving him bloodied and dazed. It wasn't just the casual violence that shocked him, it was the primal, covetous attitude to the water that left him cold. There was a custodial atmosphere out on the water: it was all about not making mistakes and giving nothing away. By then Skajarowski had become a natural bodyboarder, skimming waves in a nonchalant, intuitive way that disguised the difficulty of the form.

That year he spent travelling has left a residue of restlessness, but he has come to love Clare. 'I feel settled here,' he says. 'I've had a girlfriend here for the past three years and definitely she has kept me here.' Sometimes on visits home to Cornwall he will meet with friends who jumped straight into a career after graduation. 'And they might have bucketloads of cash. And sometimes I think that would be all right. If I wasn't into surfing, I probably would have done that too. But surfing . . . it is my form of release. Three or four years ago I needed to be in the water every day. Now I go when I need to. But in the summer, when I'm in the café and I know I have missed a good day, I feel hacked off.'

It took him over half a year to recover from his shattered knee. His 'rescue' from Riley's quickly passed into folklore. After Steph made the phone call, they waited, not really believing that anyone would turn up. Then two rescue boats appeared on the horizon and, to their amazement, a Dauphin helicopter came roaring across the sky. It hovered above them – 'Just like the films,' Skajarowski remarks with a smile. 'I remember thinking: oh God, this is going to cost a bomb. But

I was in so much pain I didn't care.' As it turned out he had to be winched into the chopper. He felt almost curious and interested in the process as he watched his saviour descend from the Dauphin overhead. A loop was slipped around his head and under his arm – 'the sausage roll thing they use to get dead bodies out' – and his rescuer warned him that he was going to feel unholy pain once they hit the side of the helicopter. His legs began to cramp up as they lifted him into the cabin.

Steph and Seamus watched on from the rocks, fascinated and aghast. 'You could hear him screaming over the helicopter,' Steph says. 'It was terrible.' Then they gathered their stuff and trudged across the fields to where their cars were parked.

Dan Skajarowksi spent a week in hospital. Tom Gillespie called in to visit him one day and was greeted with a dopey grin and a familiar 'R-roight boys!' 'I thought: same old Dan,' Gillespie remembers. 'It took me a few minutes to realize that he was out of it on morphine.'

It was a full seven months before Dan felt confident enough to take to the water again. The promise of a good swell at Aileen's was enough to lure him back. He went out with about eight other bodyboarders, including Piran, who was visiting from Cornwall. It was a gorgeous day and the swell produced regular sets of waves of between eight and ten feet high – perfect for him to shake off the cobwebs. They had been out for four hours and were thinking of spending the evening at Riley's when a six-foot wave appeared at the front of a set and everyone dived on it. Skajarowski, though, had been on the very edge of the set and missed it. He paddled hard, attempting to catch the next wave, but it broke before he reached it and he knew that he had managed to end up where he shouldn't be, caught inside the wave, facing the vast wall of the cliffs, uncertain of what was coming down the tracks.

He heard the drone of the jet-ski coming towards him and knew that whoever was driving it was pre-empting trouble. 'I just had this terrible feeling,' he remembers.

He managed to tunnel through the first wave that came, and when he resurfaced he saw a magnificent wave just forming in front of him, about twenty feet high on its face with a gorgeous, empty cavern. He paddled ferociously hard to his right, willing himself to make it around the shoulder of the wave. But it reared and broke just metres from where he floated, deafening and much more breathtakingly powerful than even he could have guessed. It wasn't like being hit by water. He was sent to the ocean floor as quickly as if he had fallen down an elevator shaft, tonnes and tonnes of sea water driving him down.

Even the most chatty of surfers tend to hesitate when they are describing the more harrowing moments they have spent wrestling with ocean currents. Dan can't recall the sensation of hitting the seabed because he was getting churned around by the wave; his body became part of the mechanics of the wave as it worked out its natural lifespan. But he was so cut up and bashed when he came up that he knows he must have been on the ocean floor for a good few seconds. He was probably under water for fifteen seconds. That is a considerable time even if you are just skimming along the tiles of a placid swimming pool. When you are already exhausted after four hours' riding big waves and have been winded by a collapsing structure of water and it's dark and cold and you can hear nothing but water fizzing in your ears and maybe even your own beating heart, it can seem like an eternity.

When the water turned heavenly green and he knew he was rising towards the surface, he braced himself for the deluge of the next wave which would surely send him down again. He had only experienced a two-wave hold-down once before and it was a place he never wanted to go again, especially at Aileen's, where the waves plough so deeply beneath the surface that the chances of not coming up, of breathing in, are significantly higher. Instead, someone – he still isn't sure who – reached in, dragged him on to the surf-ski and rushed him out of the channel while he coughed and spluttered. It was a rough return to surfing.

'Aileen's was the first time I'd got caught up in a dodgy situation for a long, long time. That [knee] injury did make me question the whole thing. I've had friends break backs and injure themselves seriously enough to quit. It took me a while to get my confidence back.'

But when he hit the water on this afternoon at Riley's he had lost all of that hesitancy, ripping through and turning 360s and disappearing into barrels, seemingly lost only to come bolting through the concave wall even as the wave collapsed. The waves were ten to twelve feet and clean and the sunshine lit the waves as they rose so that they had a deeply pure emerald colour. Standing on the cliff gives the best perspective of the scale of the wave and of how hazardously close to the reef it breaks and there were three or four photographers nestled into grassy hollows for the afternoon with long-lens cameras trained on the action. There must have been twenty people down there in all, a few out-of-towners among them: whatever secrecy there used to be about the location of Riley's is fast disappearing. But it remains stubbornly awkward to reach, with the long trek parallel along the cliff where you jump several hedges ornamented with barbed wire and pass a bemused herd of cows and a field of horses, and the walk across the base of the cliff which is littered with falling rocks and debris, past the remains of the horse and foal.

The Clare lads were at their usual spot, ditching their carrier bags beside a stack of rock that can double as bleachers: you can sit there just a stone's throw from the wave. Tom Gillespie, who had been in the water for hours, stood looking out. His lips were blue but he didn't seem to notice as he watched his friends. When Gillespie's hair is wet you can just see the long snaking scar he acquired during an accident at the Bumbaloids wave near Spanish Point. Like Skajarowski, his fall occurred from the kind of wave he has successfully ridden a thousand times. His brother Fintan was there and a friend of theirs was taking photographs. It was a sublime day and their shouts of joy seemed to carry for miles: they felt as if they had the country to themselves. 'I was a bit too cocky, to be honest,' Gillespie says with a shrug. 'It was one of the smaller waves of that session and I fell off somehow and kind of nosedived into the water. It was just really shallow there and I heard the loudest crack. There was no pain, just complete adrenalin. I was shouting for my brother and he thought I was calling him into a wave.'

Gillespie was no novice. His introduction to surfing was similar to Fergal Smith's: he happened upon a surfboard when he was with his family one summer in Louisburgh. It was one of the old-fashioned wooden planks, practically an antique, but that was the beginning for him. By the time he reached his teens he was taking day trips to Clare with Fintan. Sometimes they persuaded their mother Deirdre to drive them across the country. Most of what they knew they gleaned from magazines and from trial and error. They bumped into Andrew Kilfeather and Seamus McGoldrick one day and one set regarded the other with mutual suspicion. 'I remember Shambles saying, "Who the fuck is this Dublin lad?"' Gillespie laughs. 'But we kept an eye on weather charts and kept showing up and I suppose they could see we were serious about it.'

At the age of seventeen Gillespie was beginning to take part in competitions, and he developed a reputation for being a fearless bodyboarder. He would reappear at his school, where rugby was the dominant sport, and struggle to explain to his friends what it was that drew him to Clare or Donegal weekend after weekend. 'Eventually they would just tell me to shut up. You have to keep it to yourself.'

He met Mickey Smith and found a person completely at odds with the caricature he had begun to read about in the English surf publications. 'I thought he would be this mad bastard. What Mickey did has just opened up the potential for Irish surfing. None of these waves would have been surfed, or at least not in this way, if Mickey hadn't been here. As far as I understand, his real passion is documenting it all. He is practically ocean dwelling. He just loves being out there on the sea with a camera. He puts pressure on you in a good way. It is not that he is fearless; he is calculating. If he thinks you are going to get smashed by a wave, he doesn't want you going for it.'

But Gillespie never really needed much encouragement to go for broke on a wave. So when he stood up and turned to face Fintan that day at Bumbaloids, he absorbed the severity of his injury by reading the horror on his brother's face. His forehead had been gashed open and his face was a river of blood. Once again the remoteness of the wave's location was never so apparent. Someone phoned an ambulance to meet them at the road, but Gillespie still had to walk up a country lane in a wetsuit with blood gushing from his forehead, the cows watching stoically and enjoying the sunshine. He felt a bit ridiculous, as if he were in a mixed-up dream. An ambulance siren broke the peace, and just like that he was whisked off into the Irish healthcare system. On the way into Miltown Malbay the paramedics were wonderful, though they made the mistake of attempting to cut off his wetsuit with scissors. Gillespie wouldn't hear of it: this was a pretty new suit and he was a smashed broke student.

They decided the injury needed treatment in Galway so he was transferred up there by ambulance, and by now the pain was beginning to set in. It felt like the top of his head had been cleaved – mainly because it had. Once he had been examined in Galway he heard the doctors mentioning severe lacerations and plastic surgery. After what seemed like an interminable wait he was told that he would be seen in St James's Hospital as there were no beds in Galway. Friends drove him to Dublin and it was well after midnight when he arrived home.

He went into St James's with his father the next morning and was dispatched to another waiting room. His choice was to wait for an operating theatre to become free or to have the injury treated by local anaesthetic. 'In fairness, they had guys coming in with work injuries – carpenters who had gotten hurt. Some surfer landing in on them was going to get low priority.' He decided that he could bear the pain and just remembers digging fingernails into his hands and trying not to scream through the ordeal. He didn't even have the satisfaction of having a preposterous number of stitches to boast about: instead, one long wavy stitch was used to make the scar less obvious. He passed out three times, from exhaustion as much as pain.

The scar line is long and meandering but was so well treated that it can't be noticed clearly unless Gillespie pulls back the curtain of blond hair from his forehead. But it is a lifetime memento of what can happen just by falling the wrong way. 'It never put me off surfing but I am more wary. You just have to be conscious that these things can happen. You know, this guy from Oz fell at Bumbaloids and came up with a kind of stab wound in his side. He had been impaled under the water for a few seconds. Never happened to anyone before or since. Another of the Aussie lads got pushed into a cavern by a wave and couldn't get out. It can all go wrong quickly.'

They all assure themselves that they are careful, but sometimes the anticipation can overshadow everything else. Hugo Galloway occasionally thinks about the morning they met up on the pier in Doolin to jet-ski over to Riley's. Galloway had just completed his usual trick of leaving Galway at four in the morning. Driving through the Burren at that hour can be a disquieting experience in the height of summer, but on that morning, pitch black and shrouded in the heaviest fog, it was eerie. He knows the road by heart now, and that helped. It was bright by the time they had the skis ready and the boards unloaded from the van and they set off having convinced themselves that the fog would soon lift – it always did.

Galloway and Steph Skajarowski were on one ski; Fergal, Mickey and Tom Lowe set off on the other. All the usual coordinates were invisible: the water and the fog merged and within minutes they had lost each other. 'We just kept heading out and instead of easing up it became thicker and thicker,' Galloway recalled on a frigid day sitting outside a café near the college in Galway. He rolled a neat cigarette as he spoke and pointed to the stone wall of the college across the road. 'You could just about see that far. No more. Our logic was that it would be easier to keep going and find our way than to turn back and try and retrace our path.' They were driving blind, trying to plot their way using wind and swell direction. As well as they knew that patch of coast, it was just educated guesswork. 'Every so often we would see a rock jutting out and just wait to go hammering into something. And then the odd big wave would come at us from the side. You wouldn't know they were there until the last second. So we would adjust and try and steer around that set. Steph was driving. I had lost my mind at that stage.'

The entire misadventure probably lasted no more than half an hour, but, much like being under water, time measured itself differently. They felt completely at the mercy of the ocean.

At Riley's there is a gap where some of the cliff face has fallen away, leaving a fifty-foot obelisk rearing out of the water. It rises like an intimidating monument to the place. Its shape was discernible through the fog. Steph steered them towards it. Hugo was just delighted that they were heading towards land again. As they went through the gap they were met with a vicious wave and Steph had to turn the throttle to punch through it.

Once they had found a place to rest they realized that there was no sign of the others. For what seemed like an eternity they sat bobbing on the ski, hearing the waves but not quite seeing them, and catching hazy glimpses of the cliff line and grass verge as the fog finally began to lift. 'We were worried. We knew they wouldn't panic but, you know, those skis can tip.' Then they heard a faint drone, becoming louder by the second. They watched as the second ski shot through the gap in the cliffs. Fergal was driving and was punching the air with his fist, like Ayrton Senna at the end of a Grand Prix. He was screaming in exultation because he had seen the other ski. It had worked out fine. They waited until they could just about see the waves breaking and then went surfing.

A few months later, Hugo and Steph were riding in a ski with George Franklin, an English surfer. They were leaving Aileen's after a terrific session: Galloway had safely made his two biggest waves there and felt elated. As usual they had probably dallied a quarter of an hour too long. It never failed to surprise them just how fast the light fades there in winter: once the sun dips, the cliffs seem to retreat into a vague shadow within minutes. There was a snappy wind of about thirty knots that day so they had launched from the pier at Liscannor rather than in Doolin. The journey involved jetting around the headland and crossing an open expanse of water. It had been fine earlier in the morning but now a southeast wind blew straight across them, producing a series of choppy four- and five-foot waves which seemed intent on knocking them over. Again Galloway had that hollow feeling as Steph slowed the ski down to minimum throttle so they could hurdle the waves that came at them in steady, spiteful sets.

Soon the coastline was lit with houselights and they guessed they were about two miles out. The fuel gauge was running low and nobody had a mobile phone. Jet-skis are temperamental machines at the best of times; if this one failed them, they were goosed. George Franklin said, 'We could be fucking boned here,' and nobody spoke after that. The tide would have washed them out past Kilstephen reef in ten minutes.

The three men stayed silent and concentrated on just getting through the next wave and inching towards the pier. There was debris in the water and it sounded as if seaweed or maybe a plastic bag had become entangled in the propeller. They kept willing the ski on, feeling much further removed from their life than the fifteen-minute ride that separated them from safety. Behind them was the Atlantic, drawing them out, and they shared the unspoken knowledge that nobody knew they were out there. What Hugo remembers most vividly is the extreme coldness of the water against his knuckles every time they punched through a wave on the jet-ski.

Gradually, the harbour materialized. The relief Hugo felt at that moment was as warm and intense as whiskey. He thought about it all the way home, about just how easily it could have turned stupid and tragic. 'If you panic on the sea, you are screwed. I learned a big lesson that day. But the most frightening experience I ever had in the water wasn't even that dangerous at all. It was at home in Tramore and I got caught in a rip current and I was being dragged out a bit. I was only eleven and there were people around to help me so I was never in any real danger. But that was as scared as I have ever been, just for those few moments.'

The afternoon Dan spent at Riley's two years after he shattered his knee went without a hitch. But they all have those fears and close calls and they use them as charms to ward off the bad luck and stupid accidents that strike randomly and when least expected.

6

Northern Lights

The arrangement was to meet at Fergal Smith's house at four in the morning on 12 December. For the previous two days he and Tom Lowe had been on the phone poring over the online weather charts and speculating about a storm front that was moving across Ireland and the British Isles. Tom was down in the Canaries and was dubious about coming over until the very last minute. It was the usual dilemma. Should he tear up to the airport and pay fool's gold for a late flight into Shannon? But to be stuck down in the sunshine hearing of a glorious storm off the Irish coast would be too much to cope with.

Tom was wrecked but punctual nonetheless. Mickey, whose partner, Riv, had given birth just a fortnight earlier, was exhausted but also on time. Fergal was, as always, ready to move. So they yawned and made tea and looked out the window, waiting for headlights against the black sky to announce the arrival of The Most Laid Back Man In The World.

'Sometimes we tell Dan that we are leaving half an hour earlier than we really want to,' Mickey says. 'But he still manages to show up late. The thing is, you can't stay angry at him.'

Eventually there were the headlights, marking out the winding road against the dark landscape. They were in the van and waiting when Dan emerged from his car, cheerful and sleepy. 'R-roight boys!'

Fergal drove Mickey's van. They were heading to Mullaghmore, the wave off the Sligo coast which had a tendency to go volcanic once or twice each winter. Fergal more or less instructed Mickey to try and get some sleep in the back. Dan dozed off fairly sharply, so Fergal and Tom sat up front, driving over the Burren at that time of night when the sky is blackest. If it felt like they were the only people moving in west Clare, it is because they probably were.

Mickey lay down in the rear of the van but sleep was impossible on such a bumpy windy road. He has the habits of an insomniac at the best of times, and because he and Riv were just getting into a routine with Eiva, their infant daughter, he could have done without the demands of Mullaghmore. The swell couldn't have materialized at a more awkward time, but he felt he couldn't miss it. 'I just lay there listening to the boys. Tom and Fergal just cut each other down loads. It seems to be their way of dealing with things. Even though they are very different people, what they want is exactly the same. So I was just listening to them bantering and then every so often Dan would come throw in his tuppence worth. He won't say anything for maybe an hour and then just come out with some weird, wise phrase that will just silence everyone. Like, I think they were talking about what we were going to do when we got to Mullaghmore. There were four of us and we had just one ski so the boys were talking about someone having to paddle out alongside the ski. And Dan had been quiet and then he just comes out with: "Leave no man behind." And the thing was, we listened to him. We ended up going out with four of us in the ski in this howling wind and massive swell.'

On the radio the weather bulletins were fizzing with dramatic warnings about the state of the ocean over the coming twelve hours: storm conditions expected on all seas, and the Met Office had already measured a 20.4-metre wave off the Donegal coast.

But first they had to go through the usual complications. They picked Kevin Smith up at Charlestown and spent the drive to Sligo discussing what they should do about a camera. Fergal had just paid almost €3,000 for new equipment but was still waiting on its delivery. Tom had left the camera they usually used in Spain, and Mickey's regular film colleague Alan 'Willie' Wilson was using the other on a shoot in England. To complicate matters, they discovered as they drove that they had no battery for the one camera they had with them. They realized they were going to have to search in Sligo for one. So they unhitched the jet-ski from the rear of the van and left it with Tom and Dan on a grass verge off a dual carriageway. This was before nine on a wild December morning. The two boys sat there wrapped in hats and staring back at the commuters, who gave them strange looks as they passed by.

Fergal and Mickey did a tour of the appliances shops in Sligo but failed to locate a replacement battery. They decided there was nothing for it but to buy a camera. 'We only needed it for this one day so we didn't want to do it,' Fergal said. 'We figured we would try and flog it on eBay or something.' As it happened, he got a phone call from one of his surfing sponsors while he was in the shop. They were keen for him to be in Mullaghmore and wanted to make sure he had film. Fergal explained that they had no choice but to buy new equipment and was given the go-ahead. By the time they collected the jet-ski and the two boys it was close on ten in the morning: they had been travelling for six hours and the day was only just beginning.

Mullaghmore was in godly mood that morning. For decades the place was best known as a pleasant fishing village with a fabulous beach, and it was periodically mentioned as the location of one of the darker episodes in the history of the Troubles, when Lord Mountbatten and others were killed by an IRA bomb on a late August morning in 1979 after setting out for a day's fishing in the *Shadow V*, a simple fishing boat that had been moored in the harbour. But in recent years Mullaghmore has become celebrated for its waves.

Local surfers had always used the reefs there but the revelation of the existence of a giant wave, soon known as Prowler's, in the winter of 2010 generated immense publicity for the area. The wave had in fact been known about for some time and local winter surfers had been biding their time, waiting for optimum conditions. The tail end of Hurricane Thomas facilitated unprecedented swells, and on 10 November six surfers set off for the wave, located some two miles off shore. It was a multinational expedition, with surfers from Ireland, England and South Africa. By the following evening the discovery of a huge virgin wave off the northwest had made it on to the main evening news, emphasizing another coup for Irish surfing and local tourism; reports about the size of the wave appeared on numerous websites and in film footage soon afterwards. The group who had pioneered the wave were initially coy about its precise coordinates and were helped by the fact that it was so far off shore. But the only way they could keep the wave to themselves was to sign a covenant swearing one another to secrecy, and they knew that would prove futile. So, just like that, Prowler's entered the big-wave lexicon. It was another example of just how far removed surfing had got from the old days when knowledge about waves in remote locations spread like Chinese whispers. Now it was instant and everywhere, all at once.

But Prowler's was not the objective on this day. Big, high-quality barrels were forming much closer to shore at Mullaghmore Head. Shortly after the Clare boys arrived they saw Jayce Robinson, a surfer from St Ives in Cornwall, sitting in his van. They shouted a quick hello and continued getting ready. Robinson had briefly and spectacularly ridden into the teeth of a break that was later estimated to have risen to sixty-seven feet. He was an accomplished surfer but a relative novice on big waves and was not all that familiar with Mullaghmore. He had surfed the water there for the first time the previous evening and had come back early that morning with Lyndon Wake, his tow-in partner. The waves he'd towed into became incrementally bigger and he later confessed that he'd had no idea of just how gargantuan the final wave he rode into was until he cast an eye skyward and saw the lip hanging above him and it was like nothing he had ever seen before. He probably had half a second to absorb the fact that he was going to get obliterated, and on television afterwards he described the experience as comparable to 'being in a washing machine'. 'It was definitely the biggest barrel I've ever surfed,' he told *Sky News*. 'I was a little nervous but I didn't have time to think about it – it's like a car crash, you almost don't know what's happening.' Robinson dislocated his knee and his board snapped in two, but the price was relatively light given the force of the wave and the flashbulb aftermath of his tale.

The Clare lads knew nothing of this when they went into the water. By mid-morning the swell had attracted a notable selection of experienced local surfers. Richie Fitzgerald, one of the leading lights of the Irish surfing movement and one of those who had pioneered Prowler's, was already out there. Neil Britton, whose father Brian and uncles had been surfing in Rossnowlagh during the years when surfing was marginally more popular than moon-walking, was also there. Paul O'Kane, an Australian with effervescent energy and four decades of surfing to his name, was out there too. Surf-skis cut through the white water and circled around the breaking waves, and from the grass verge overlooking Mullaghmore photographers and film makers chronicled the session.

The Clare group, mindful of Dan's credo, set off together, hanging off their single jet-ski, equipment everywhere. Mickey was content just to ride the jet-ski for the morning, filming the three boys, acting as a safety runner and a kind of advance scout. Fergal and Tom's plan was to spend the session trying to paddle into the waves. Their belief was that the scale and quality of the breaks made that just about possible. As ever, the pair were completely different in their approach. Fergal was both tentative and completely calm. The waves were of a quality that only appears once or twice a winter, giving him a chance to test the limits of his skill in paddling into a wave with which he wasn't that well acquainted. His one regret was that he had not heeded the advice of John 'JP' Purton, his board-shaper, who had crafted the board which he was now riding specifically for this wave. 'Try it out before you go there,' he had said, but Smith hadn't had the chance to do so. So now he was on an eight-foot board rather than his customary board, which measures 5ft 9in. It was an inch thicker as well, and it felt unwieldy underneath him, like steering a boat whose rudder isn't working. It took him a full hour just to gain confidence in it and to feel it out and gauge its nuances until it at least began to feel as if it were a part of him. Tom was, as ever, gung-ho, exhilarated by the quality of the charging waves and delighted that he had made the trip up from the Canaries.

Smith and Lowe were the only surfers who were paddling that morning. All around them the others were glorying in the frequency and quality of the waves and one by one Fitzgerald, Britton, Tom Butler, Dylan Stott, Gareth Marshall and Barry Mottershead caught waves that they would remember. From the shore, the tableau looked terrific: surf-skis skirting around the fringes of beautifully sculpted, lunatic waves and every so often the pencil-thin silhouettes of surfers somehow cutting through them before, more often than not, vanishing in a snarl of white water. But the day also brought home the friction that has always existed between paddle-in and tow-in surfing.

The advent of tow-in surfing transformed the possibilities of big wave surfing. The concept was drifting around as an idea since the 1960s but was only put into sound practice in the 1990s in Oahu when the Hawaiian surfers Laird Hamilton, Buzzy Kerbox and Darrick Doerner began using an inflatable

Zodiac boat to tow one another into waves measuring around fifteen feet. From there they graduated to the Jaws wave in Maui and were soon tinkering with modifications like foot-straps and faster jet-skis. Over the coming years the trio successfully towed into and surfed waves of monstrous proportions which gripped an audience that transcended the traditional surfing community.

The advantages of the tow-in method – greater speed and flexible take-off positions – were so obvious that the only question was why surfers had taken so long to adapt it. Within five years the sight of surfers trailing behind a ski-rope became common. But even as the practice was hailed for the freedom and velocity it gave the most daring and accomplished big wave riders interested in harnessing ridiculously massive slabs of water, there was a counter argument: it was the antithesis of surfing, where threading the eye of the needle of a wave even as it reared and formed was the essence of the art, surfing it the incidental reward.

Smith and Lowe are hardly paddle-in purists: they have towed into waves countless times. The appeal of this day in Mullaghmore was that the waves were of a size Fergal had daydreamed about countless times. 'That day in December was the limit in terms of paddling. It was the optimum size and it was as close to the day that I have often thought about – fifteen foot, good winds and perfect times – as you could get. There were so many waves coming in that were paddleable. I spent a lot of the time just sitting there and it was killing me, watching those waves go by. But that is the learning curve, just going through that stage of waiting and learning what you can do.'

Opting to paddle in was Smith and Lowe's prerogative. Equally, using the skis was the absolute right of the other surfers on the water. The tricky part was keeping some semblance of order: with so many skis scooting about the surf to drop their passengers into a wave or to collect them before another wave smashed down on them, and with the waves breaking thunderously and the wind roaring in ears, it was hard for everyone to keep track of who was doing what and when. Mickey Smith spent most of the time sitting back on his ski parallel to the break of the waves so he could see the sets of waves as they began to form and also what occurred over the falls. Because it was so busy he had an uneasy feeling. 'It was just fucking heavy that day . . . a lot of people and a lot going on.' His fear was that once Fergal or Tom committed to a wave, they would be clueless as to what was materializing around them.

Surf-skis are deceptive: they have this association with frivolity and pleasure-seeking but they are heavy-duty and potentially lethal machines – half a tonne of metal cutting across the ocean surface. Mullaghmore on wilder days has proved a graveyard for several skis.

Mickey Smith was keeping an eye on Tom as he began that liquid-smooth transition from paddling to dropping down the face of a wave. Lowe has a style that is entirely his own. He has the frame of a sprinter and seems to establish himself on the board with maximum efficiency, but once he has chosen a line through the wave he becomes slope-shouldered and nonchalant. Mickey kept watching him and was delighted to see Lowe's success, but almost at the same time he saw a jet-ski as it was thrown over the falls and two heads going

161

over with it into the waves. All of this happened in a matter of seconds, and by the time Mickey had processed the worry that Tom's line was on a collision course with the ski, it had already happened. 'I just saw Tom's board pop up like a sky tombstone, and then he pops up so I went and got him.'

Tom Lowe had seen the ski at the very last second – the machine was white and camouflaged by the soupy water in the end bowl of the wave. On instinct he just hurled himself off the board and arrowed through the water underneath the machine. The ski was tossed around in the water as if it was a bath toy. 'I've never seen Lowey shaken about anything, ever,' Smith says. 'But he was fucking crazy that day. He got off lightly. But you know, after a few moments he got his breath back and just said fuck it and went again. Anyone else would have been put off for life.'

It was just one of those things. By then they were all aware that it was one of those God-given days when the rest of the country was huddled inside or, at best, marvelling at the waves from the safety of a coastal path while they were out there hurling themselves into the elements. Surfers are geeky about big-day dates the way some people are religious about birth-dates. The numerals of special days become burnt on to their retinas: 12-12-2011 was already one such date and it wasn't even lunchtime.

Fergal continued to wrestle with his frustrations. It was the same for Dan. Fergal had watched Dan's gradual transformation from a meek-mannered bodyboarder into the one person in their group who seemed more often than not to land the choice wave of the afternoon. 'Dan's a funny one. He's like this silent charger. He doesn't do anything for ages and then all of a sudden, it happens. Dan will always find the gem, always. He will be in the most critical spot on the wave and get the heaviest barrel. But he is not the kind of guy to force a situation. The thing about Mullaghmore is that it's quite safe as it goes because it has deep water all around it. It just takes a while to learn the ins and outs, and I reckon the next time he is out there in waves like that he will get a lot more.'

Fergal stayed out in the water for over three hours and came away having at least felt that he had managed to paddle into a few half-decent waves. 'I was second guessing myself the whole time. But I didn't mind that because we were all just buzzing to be out there. You know, to have fifteen-foot waves but being able to surf them as if they were two-footers – you could take off, bottom turn, pull into the barrel and potentially come out. I know how rarely those conditions appear on the whole planet, let alone in Ireland. For whatever reason, I wasn't ready for a big part of it. I suppose I needed to have surfed the board. By the end of the session I loved that board and I know now that I can surf it. But for the early part the feeling was just: I'm scared, I'm scared . . .'

One of Fergal Smith's quirks is that he wears his fear easily. He has developed an international reputation for fearlessness but readily confesses the opposite. Countless times he has been driven to the seabed and into reefs after getting caught in front of a breaking wave. Tens of thousands of people have seen the film where he gets punished for a reckless moment in Teehopou, when his mistake was apparent even before he had made it; all he could do was attempt to stand on his board to confirm to himself that where he was on the wave meant surfing was out of the question, and then instantly switch into survival mode, leaping off the board and falling kind of daintily down the face of the turquoise wall of water that would drive him into the coral and hammer his knee badly. At least Mullaghmore didn't have jagged coral beneath the surface. Given a similar misjudgement, the chances are that he would have been fine. But Smith has learned to walk this fine line between courage and scrupulous calculation every single time. When he decides to go for a wave it is with a combination of battle-charge blood rush and mathematical conviction that his judgement is as sound as it can possibly be.

'You need to have 100 per cent faith and commitment to that decision and if anything is preventing you, you just don't do it,' he explains. 'When you go, you do say that in your mind . . . Fuck it! But it is not about that. It is about seeing it happen to the point where it feels as if it is definitely going to work. And it takes a long time for me. I got one really good wave in the whole session that day [at Mullaghmore]. I got right in the sweet perfect position and I dropped in and the board clicked. It felt perfect. I had caught a few smaller waves and it felt like a boat. It was pretty foreign, the whole feeling. But when I was in the right spot in a wave that the board was made for, everything just fitted. Eight foot isn't that long for a big wave and it's easy to turn and it did, it turned really well at the bottom. For that wave I bombed right into the barrel, but there was something weird in the lip line, this chunk of water that wasn't perfect. And it sent down loads of spray so I wasn't going to make it. But I didn't care. The board worked. I got smashed but it was fine.'

In the film taken that day, at the moment Lowe and Smith are crouched on the boards at the apex of the wave they look terribly fragile. They look like ordinary people, in other words, summiting a rearing body of water for a nanosecond. In one wave Lowe crouches on the board and skates along the lip for half a second and then the entire construct gives way beneath him and he disappears into a Niagara of white water, arms flailing. For the one wave Smith was satisfied with, he takes an acute line down the steep face and races along its base. For one second he is plainly visible against a green Atlantic backdrop, then in the blink of an eye he is gone as the wave wraps a hollowed cloak around him. That split second when the water is like a canopy above him and the daylight begins to disappear and it feels like the world has been reduced to nothing but him and this wave, a wave he knows he has read perfectly, and that he has a decent chance of coming out the far side: that is what he is looking for every time.

Mickey was caught between losing himself in filming Fergal and remaining mindful of his primary duty of collecting him. He found it hard to estimate the size of the waves and still does. The previous winter they had been there with Rusty Long, the Californian, who described it as fifty to sixty feet. 'Where he's from, everything is measured by the face. We go by . . . the feeling in the water. We had wanted to do that for so long and it is fucking dangerous. There were twenty-foot waves coming through the line-up. But only a couple of them, you know. It is pretty weird when waves get that big and are still hollow, not just big fat waves, they are long and what not. It becomes hard to put a size on them.' Whatever the exact measurement, one thing was for sure: they were frighteningly big.

By the time the session was over they were exhausted, and

they still faced a long drive back to Clare. They were happier about what the day promised for the future rather than the waves they surfed. They would give the footage to Analog and move on. They stopped at a farmer's store they know of near Markree Castle and grabbed buckwheat, olives and apricots, hot drinks and nuts. 'Anything we could get our hands on,' Fergal laughs. 'Everyone was delirious with tiredness but we were happy. Nobody felt as if we did anything ground-breaking but we tried to give it a go.'

It was darkening again by the time they reached home and went through the monotony of unpacking everything, another day down. Over the following days they learned of Jayce Robinson's extravagant introduction to mega-wave surfing when a photograph began to appear on the major news websites capturing the surfer just before the wave engulfed him. The television report estimated that it had been the largest wave ever surfed in Ireland.

Only a few months later Robinson's claim was eclipsed. In the early days of March 2012 the weather charts and online surf pages highlighted a storm front moving down from Green-land that promised to brew up a raucous day at Mullaghmore. Thursday 8 March was regarded as the red letter day.

'It's definitely going to be huge,' Fergal Smith had said on the phone a few days beforehand. 'Just not sure if it's going to be any good.'

Once again Tom Lowe found himself boarding an evening flight out of Lanzarote to Shannon. Fergal collected him, and on the drive over to Lahinch they discussed where to surf the following morning. Fergal had an instinctive feeling that there would be better waves breaking locally and knew that they would have their choice of waves all day. But they were both eager to try and paddle into Mullaghmore again, and the lure was too much. The tide was turning around midday and the charts indicated that the off-shore wind would only begin to pick up around then as well, so they left at six in the morning, reckoning that they would be in good time if they were in the water by ten.

Like most Irish seaside towns, Mullaghmore all but hangs out a closed-for-the-winter sign during the off-season. The gate at the long narrow road up to Classie Bawn, the haughty stone castle which had been the Mountbatten summer residence, was closed and decorated with the stiff advice that this was private property. The big place looked lightless. In town, the newsagent was just opening up, the pubs were still shuttered, and the tide had completely drained away, leaving four fishing boats leaning into the pier wall, balancing on their prows. In the cradle of the town you couldn't really feel the wind, but the road through the village sweeps up a steep hill and rewards sightseers with a jaw-dropping view of Donegal bay.

Even at ten in the morning, cars had been ditched on the grass banks on the crest of the hill and all the way down the slope to sea level. All eyes were directed at the water. The waves were big and mutinous and desperately squally, and in the water half a dozen jet-skis were circling about, the riders trying to make sense of the patterns and to read the lines. Most of them were still sharing the adrenalin of what proved to be the most spectacular surf of the day.

Fergal, Tom and Mickey arrived in Mullaghmore just

seconds before Andrew Cotton, the Devon surfer, was towed into a wave that seemed to have been created by Hollywood special effects rather than a northwest Irish tidal swell. The wave disguised itself: there was no way of telling how monstrous it was going to be until Cotton had let go of the rope and straightened up. Even as Al Mennie, his tow-in partner, disappeared over the back, it began to fully form, and it was like a creature rising from the water rather than the water itself. Within two seconds Cotton had surfed a line down to the base of the wave and angled left before cutting back up the slope and running with the break. Several cameras were filming him on shore, and in the clips that began to appear online afterwards you can hear the thrill and terror in the voices as they assess the size of the wave and compare it to the size of the man. Mennie would later admit that after he had towed his friend into the wave he had time to briefly turn his head, and when he saw what was about to transpire he yelled, 'Oh fuck, Cotty!'

The chances were that Cotton couldn't hear him above the wave noise, but there was nothing he could have done anyway. It was clear that Cotton had got himself entangled with a wave that seemed to belong to the surfing book of rumour and exaggeration. It bucked so hard and so quickly that it was hard to believe it wasn't just an apparition. But there it was, at six minutes past ten in the morning, clear as day. For three or four seconds Cotton enjoyed one of the most sublime experiences of his surfing life, hurtling along on this oceanic energy form that he had managed to harness and not having to think about anything much other than the second ahead – other than staying on his board and feeling and hearing the canopy of water arc over his head and the white water crashing behind him, eating up the smooth wall of water and threatening to engulf him.

Spectators just about had time to idly wonder if he was going to make it when it became clear that he wasn't. There is always this split-second transition, when the surfer, who seems to be gliding across the face of the wave so perfectly that he creates the illusion of being in control, is suddenly at its mercy. The structure of the wave begins to fold in on him, or he loses that crucial bit of speed, or he has taken a line that is slightly wrong and then there is nothing he can do but surrender to its natural course. In Cotton's case in Mullaghmore, this meant disappearing into a furious tornado of white water and then waiting for the real weight and power of the wave – tonnes and tonnes of icy, beautifully clean Atlantic water – to crash down on him.

It was quite a moment for the thirty-two-year-old. He had camped at Mullaghmore the previous night with Mennie, so they had the place to themselves in the morning. The duo had made headlines the previous December when Mennie towed the Hawaiian surfer Garrett McNamara into a laughably big wave in Portugal. It is ranked, in the imperfect science of wave measurement, at ninety feet, thereby making it the biggest wave ever surfed. But by the spring, Mike Parson's feat at Cortes Banks still stood as the official record. Mennie, tall and flame-bearded, cuts a distinctive figure in the surf community and for ten years he has been relentless in the pursuit of big waves. Cotton was no stranger to Mullaghmore either: it was the first Irish wave he had surfed after Mennie had persuaded him to come over and he knew how capricious it could be. 'All these swells that hit Ireland can be hit and miss with wind and this one couldn't make its mind up,' Cotton would say. 'I've spent so many swells on that headland with the wind howling but not quite in the right direction and I honestly thought that this was going to be another swell like that.'

The origins of the unruly sets of breakers could be traced back to hurricane-force winds blowing south for a thousand miles from the southern tip of Greenland. Their full fury was directed at the western coast of Scotland, but the northwest of Ireland got the rough surf without the unruly winds. The waves coming in were mountainous in size and structure. After trying to gauge it for half an hour, the pair decided they might as well get in the water. Cotton's timing was perfect: had they skied out five minutes later he would have missed that wave. And he wasn't even supposed to be there. After hanging around Bundoran for three months waiting for a day like this, he had cancelled plans to leave at the last minute when the latest swell promised something. So minutes after wondering if the swell would yield anything at all, he found himself robbing the orchard.

Tom Lowe has known Andrew Cotton since they were teenagers coming through on the English surf scene, and he watched the Devon man surfing in pure wonderment. 'I was delighted for him,' he said afterwards. 'And I was green. It was one of the best waves I've ever seen around here.'

But that wave was peculiar: rather than signalling a barrage of epochal waves, it stood alone as a freak. The rest of the morning was unsatisfactory, the blustery sets unreadable and uneven. Mickey, Fergal and Tom skied out in the hope of resuming their aspirations to properly paddle into a notable

Mullaghmore big wave. Fergal, though, didn't hold out much hope of that happening.

Around eleven o'clock Eric Rebière, a French surfer, chanced a wave. He had flown in from Spain just for this day and after several hours of observing the waves his patience cracked. Paul O'Kane, the experienced Australian surfer who lives locally, towed him in. Rebière had reason to be fond of Mullaghmore: at a big-wave contest held there the previous February he had been towed into a wave that barrelled gorgeously for him and he surfed clean through it. This day was the flip side. The wave was messy and the tide was still quite low and Rebiere got cleaned out.

'Over the falls' may be a seemingly innocuous, even glamorous term, but being sucked up through the lip of a wave as it peaks and then slammed down on the ocean floor is horrible, and it can be dangerous – the equivalent of being spear-tackled in rugby, except that the weight of the water, the speed of the wave and the attendant panic of being held down increase the possibility of an unhappy outcome. From the shore, Rebière's wipe-out did not look all that ferocious. The water swatted him the way a grizzly might swipe at a hiker who had wandered into his path. But the real action occurred under water: the Frenchman was hammered against the seabed and cracked his ribs and was winded, and when he resurfaced he couldn't do much to fight the surf and was carried fifty metres within seconds, with O'Kane racing in on the ski to collect him and transport him to safety.

That was Rebière's day over, and his misfortune was enough to convince the others to head ashore. After that, the only person to be seen on the water was Mickey Smith, who was blissfully shooting film of the empty waves, navigating his ski with one hand and taking film with the other. ('Mickey,' sighed Steph Skajarowski one day in a voice that suggested the world isn't fair, 'is just a beautiful driver of those machines.')

Mickey Smith must have stayed out there for about an hour. And he wasn't the only one enthralled by the waves. By lunch-time quite a crowd had gathered at Mullaghmore. A sharp entrepreneur arrived and set up a stall selling hot drinks and crêpes.

After Mickey dropped them at the pier, Fergal and Tom had taken a walk along the headland just to keep moving and to look for Kevin, who had chosen a spot with a panoramic view of the entire area. They were still in their wetsuits and becoming increasingly dubious about getting any surfing done that day, and annoyed that they had missed out on that gift of a wave that broke just as they arrived. They were begin-ning to wish they had gone elsewhere. They kept looking at the coastal flags, willing the wind to change direction so it could lick some shape into the waves. Fergal was fairly certain it wasn't going to change but Tom was more optimistic: he was determined to at least try to tow into a few so that his journey wouldn't be a complete waste.

By one o'clock the water was busy again, and as the after-noon progressed the conditions became wilder. Waves came in unpredictable clusters and their effect was not unlike those scenes in old westerns when a posse of ne'er-do-wells comes riding into town, and shops shut and doors close. On the water the jet-skis lined up and one by one the surfers began to take turns towing into waves, tentatively at first but with increasing boldness as the afternoon wore on. As well as all the skis, two safety boats were positioned outside the wave for the entire afternoon. To add colour to the proceedings, a guy on a wind surfboard came careening out from the harbour. The conditions were perfect for him and he made short work of harnessing a few big waves, getting half barrelled by one or two and always game for more. His name was Finn Mullen, and for a good half hour the Armagh lad showed remarkable indifference to his own wellbeing as he stole the show. 'That was the coolest thing about the day, I reckon,' Fergal Smith would say later. 'I thought I recognized his face but I don't know him. All the other lads were delighted for him.'

One by one, all the surfers played private games of dare. Tom Lowe's patience finally snapped and he had Fergal tow him into a wave. For Lowe, the day had amounted to nothing more than a series of frustrations and he couldn't face the idea of trekking back down to the Canaries without a single wave for his troubles. He cast his mind back to the previous spring at Mullaghmore, when Fergal had towed him into a phenomenal wave. 'It was the same kind of day. Fergal stays really blasé about it . . . He just tows you in and off you go. So I was very relaxed about it all that day. I just wanted to be strong and solid and ended up making a barrel which remains the best of my life. So I was hoping that it could turn out like that again. I just wanted to get a couple! All that travelling and hanging around. I was convincing myself that the wind would turn.' The lure was irresistible – fifteen- and twenty-foot waves crashing about them. Lowe told himself that he would ride them safely. 'You can go down the edge of 'em or shoulder-ride them. But I didn't want to do that. So I figured I might get a barrel and then get out before the wave chandeliered. I got five waves and three of them barrelled and two of those landed on me.'

'Weird waves' is how Lowe would later describe their shape. But he was convinced that he could do something with them. The vicarious thrill of Andrew Cotton's wave was still burning inside him. But there was more to it as well. By mid-afternoon it was clear to everyone that Mullaghmore would go down as one of the famed days. Lowe is a professional surfer. Sponsors expect their riders to show up and be seen at gala days like this and, ideally, to produce the outstanding few seconds of highlight film of the day. With photographers and film crews now ubiquitous, all it takes is one outlandish wave and a combination of good fortune, courage and nerve for a surfer to make a wave which might get seen across the global surfing community. That can mean a difference in the next pay cheque that lands through the letter box. So there is an implicit but significant pressure on any surfer with sponsorship – or a surfer looking for sponsorship – to star in a film featuring a murderously powerful wave. And that pressure can muddy the thought process for surfers when they are judging whether or not to take on a wave; they can go against their better instinct. Fergal Smith probably knew that in the days and weeks to come his sponsors might wonder why he didn't feature in the films and photographs posted on surf sites. Lowe, too, may have felt some duty to his sponsors to at least try and paddle into one of the constructs. But he knew in his heart that those waves could not be made the way he wanted to surf them.

The second wave that slammed into Lowe came just as he was coming through the barrel. 'I hit a chop and did the splits and then went over the falls. I ended up ripping my hamstring. But I know I made the wave and I know I ran a good line . . . and that was the reason that Fergal didn't want to do it. Those waves could not be surfed properly. It smashed me and I got injured. And that is why Fergal doesn't surf on those days. He doesn't feel the need to prove himself. And the whole scene – jet-skis flying around and the cars on the hill . . . all the stuff we normally don't go to. It was a bit like Hawaii. This is Ireland. It shouldn't be like that.' But for the gathering crowd on the headland, watching the show was a splendid way to pass an afternoon. The place is like a natural amphitheatre. Gabe Davies, Richie Fitzgerald, Neil Britton and Tom Butler each took turns in towing into spectacular waves. Sebastian Steudtner, a German big wave specialist who had won the XXL competition (a kind of Oscars ceremony of the surfing world) two years earlier for a huge, slow-forming barrel he rode clean through in Maui, was out there as well. Steudtner's presence in the northwest had already been noted in the local newspapers: he had been hired by Tourism Ireland to surf the local waters for commercials that would be shown on German television. So there was an international cast.

On the grassy slope overlooking the water, the swell continued to grow as well. More and more people came. And it wasn't just surf kids. It was young mothers and grandmothers walking prams. Couples of pensionable age sat in their cars, enjoying the spectacle without feeling the brunt of the wind. There was nothing sharp about the day – it was a balmy nine degrees for early March – but the wind was strong. Parents brought children in school uniforms up once the bells went and they chased each other round on the grass, enjoying the fresh air. A neat row of photographers, amateur and otherwise, lined the headland and cast worried looks at the sunlight which became poorer after three o'clock. Someone drove a vintage jeep down to the very tip of the headland. There was a sort of a haze to the day: you couldn't see across the bay and the grey backdrop made the action on the water blurry at times. A tourist from Gloucester came tramping through the rough grass; he had been out walking and had been attracted by the crowd. He said he was visiting for a wedding and had never seen anything like this. He stared at the to-ing and fro-ing on the water with a look that said that he had seen it all now. It was as if he couldn't decide whether to disapprove or be astonished. Eventually, he broke into a grin. And this was the thing: everyone was enjoying the occasion. Dogs ran about the place and everyone seemed exhilarated and in high spirits. Whenever one of the surfers managed to survive a wave, they earned the appreciation of car horns.

Out on the water, Fergal Smith's prediction was coming true. The swell was big, but for his purposes it wasn't any good. The waves just weren't of the quality that made it possible to do anything with. By the middle of the afternoon, when they had decided to call it quits and headed back to the pier and were hauling the ski up the slope, it looked as if the wind had changed direction enough to improve the wave quality. So they relaunched the ski and joined the others again, but nothing changed. For the first time in his life, Smith spent an entire afternoon on the water without trying to surf a single wave. 'You can get barrelled but if you do, you won't make it. And that is really dangerous, so you put yourself on the line for what? A split second of being in a big tube. And that's it. I couldn't bring myself to do it. I felt I couldn't go down the wave just to do it . . . I don't care how I look but I would feel like a douche-bag for myself. The only time I feel right is when I'm in the right position – when you are in the best spot in the wave. Going down the shoulder of a wave . . . it doesn't sit well with me. I would rather not bother doing it than to just cruise down a wave for the sake of it. And I thought I might be able to practise paddling into a wave or two, but even that wasn't possible.'

It wasn't that he wanted to be churlish about the surfing that was going on around him, or that he wanted to deny his companions' right to have a good time. Part of him enjoyed the exhilaration of the scene and the immensity of the waves. But the surfer in him was lost. He had gone against his instincts by turning up for the swell and had to write the day off as a waste. He had a new board that Tom Doidge-Harrison had shaped for him specifically for a wave in Lahinch and he wanted nothing more than to try it out. But to just go for it would have been to forsake one of his strongest virtues as a surfer: his scrupulous judgement. Twice he went so far as to have Tom Lowe tow him into a wave. 'But I had a look at 'em and it just didn't feel right. And if it doesn't feel right, then you shouldn't be doing it. And I was thinking at that moment: what am I doing? This isn't me. I don't enjoy this stuff. Look, nobody wants to surf Mullaghmore more than I do. But I felt that wasn't the day for it.'

For Smith, every wave he has ever surfed has been tied into an instinctive feeling that it will work out, as if a karma descends in the crucial seconds when he decides whether or not to go with a wave. It doesn't matter where in the world he is, being patient and watchful is part of the make-up. So the spectator in him appreciated the delirium going on all around him. He could hear the howls of enthusiasm and see the excitement on people's faces, and even through the squall it was clear that a big crowd had gathered on the headland, that the afterglow of Cotton's morning wave had carried through. It was a rare day on the Irish coast. It looked beautiful. And it had succeeded in doing something that matters deeply to himself and Mickey: it got people to turn away from the town for an hour or two and become stilled by nature. No, the day was magnificent. It was just that for his interpretation of what surfing is all about, it was no good.

Not long after that the Clare lads turned for Mullaghmore pier, packed away their gear and started the long drive home in sombre mood. Nobody else noticed: they were having the time of their lives. Time and time again surfers rode the gauntlet of choppy, lazily powerful waves. Every so often a big arcing barrel of water would fall over them and then they would just disappear in a detonation of water. The white water would fan out as it died, and on the headland people would study the soupy aftermath for a bobbing surfboard and to see if the surfer was all right. People and sport are the same the world over: the possibility of violence is what thrills the audience most. Witnessing someone getting ploughed off their board was half the excitement for these people. The same contradiction lies at the heart of boxing: nobody wants to see a fighter get hurt but they show up anyway in the knowledge that that is precisely what they may see. At one point Tom Butler attempted to paddle into a wave. He appeared on its crest, a tiny, flailing, insignificant figure, and even as he dropped down he was doomed. It seemed reckless, but he got away with it.

They all did. As it turned out, Ollie O'Flaherty from Lahinch ended up generating as many headlines as Cotton. O'Flaherty was filmed as he was towed by Gabe Davies into a wave which stayed solid until he had reached its base and then simply disintegrated on top of him. Word of the day's events in Mullaghmore did not take long to navigate the globe and a brief montage featuring the most spectacular rides and wipe-outs was posted on the Magicseaweed website. Within a week the O'Flaherty video had registered a quarter of a million views – blissful numbers for clothing and board sponsors. Then, a film taken by Jamie Russell of Andrew Cotton's surf was included as a late entry in the Billabong XXL Wave of the Year competition, the annual mega-contest featuring the heaviest waves of the previous twelve months. Cotton's was placed at around fifty feet, ranking it by many estimates among the biggest waves anybody had ever surfed into. A few weeks later O'Flaherty made the shortlist along with Cotton in the Biggest Wave category. The awards were due to be held in California in May. The XXL awards are an ingenious marketing wheeze. Each category – Ride of the Year, Wipe-out of the Year, etc. – holds a prize of $50,000 for the winner (though $500,000 a man would seem more appropriate, given the exposure and profile of the scheme). Just like that, O'Flaherty was being judged with the same level of scrutiny as Garrett McNamara, the rambunctious Hawaiian who is twenty years O'Flaherty's senior. It was a dizzying rise in profile for the young Clare man, and another of those occasions when surfing proved irresistible to mainstream media in Ireland. It was one of those exotic stories which travelled and also one which highlighted the impoverishment that often goes hand-in-hand with the surfing life: as O'Flaherty explained in interviews in the days afterwards, while he was delighted with the nomination, his main concern was to try to raise enough money for his air fare to Los Angeles.

But that was all in the future. That day in Mullaghmore he was just lost in the moment.

The water was busy until five o'clock in the evening. By then, motorists had their car headlights on and the bay was beginning to twinkle with household lights.

And here is the thing. This was an ordinary Thursday afternoon in a troubled country. The hourly news bulletins on the radio delivered clipped stories that were true to the mood of the times. In Dublin, Gardai had moved to break up the Occupy Dame Street movement which had housed itself at the Central Bank of Ireland premises in the city. Allied Irish Bank confirmed that it would be cutting its workforce by 2,500 people, a staggering number of people for one company to lose – a virtual small town of clerks and managers and salespeople cast adrift in an employment market which held nothing but grim prospects. These were the major preoccupations of the day on Thursday, 8 March 2012. But for the small band of surfers on the water those thoughts were far away, at least for the hours when they were out there battling the elements. And for the audience, watching them was a distraction. Watching Finn Mullen on his manic interloping windsurfing mission that bracing spring afternoon was a form of escapism right on their doorstep. It was hard to imagine a more breathtaking setting. It wasn't just the sea that was producing a March spectacular either. Astronomy enthusiasts were looking forward to the consequences of the biggest solar storm the earth had experienced in five years: it might destroy power grids, but it would also facilitate breathtaking views of the Aurora Borealis.

Tom Butler was the last surfer to leave the water, and by then most of the crowd had begun to drift home. Evening chores beckoned. Butler caught one last wave that wasn't as towering as some of the others but wasn't as manic either, and he surfed it in a comfortable, stop-start fashion, gliding up the face of the wave and snapping down towards the trough. Just when it seemed it had run out of steam, the wave gave him an extra burst and he surfed every ounce of energy out of it as it faded. Then he left.

The patch of water felt like an arena after the performers have left the stage. The waves kept coming anyway.

It was probably Mullaghmore's last hurrah for the season.

7

Mac's, 8 a.m.

Mickey Smith was already waiting at Mac's petrol station outside Doolin when Fergal Smith pulled up in his van. It was dry and crisply cold and just after eight o'clock on a February morning. Things move gently in west Clare at this time of the day and the road was empty. As Fergal filled a container with diesel for his jet-ski, he gestured out towards the sea. 'Between those two houses,' he said brightly, pointing to where a coil of white surf was rolling on the marbled waters. 'That's Lauren's. We might end up going there.' Fergal had been up at the cliffs from about half past seven, trudging across the field to see how the wave was shaping up. The plan had been to spend the day at Aileen's, and although the weather charts looked promising, he had to see for himself. 'It's pumping,' he had reported when he returned, 'but I dunno how clean it's going to be when they break.'

Mac's was just opening for business for the day so Mickey

stood chatting with Tom Lowe and his girlfriend, Yanni, who were travelling with Fergal. The plan now was that Tom and Fergal would spend the day surfing at either Aileen's or Lauren's while Mickey concentrated on some filming work which had just been commissioned by Paramount Pictures. The previous day he had driven to Dublin to collect specialized cameras with the brief to capture venomous footage of the sea bashing against rocks and generally being malevolent. They wanted to insert it into a feature film, *Snow White and the Huntsman*.

Peculiar left-field jobs sometimes land on Mickey's lap out of the blue. He still isn't certain how they came across him but presumes someone had seen his short film *Dark Side of the Lens* online. The company had contacted him with the idea months before, had flown him to Pinewood Studios, and had originally scheduled him to shoot footage over the winter and do second-unit footage – subtle visuals – as well. 'The director of photography was buzzing,' Smith says of that original meeting. 'But what you realize is that a production like that is just a huge machine with a sliding scale of priority. When the production side of things came in, the attitude was: who are you guys and what are you doing here? So the plan of shooting for the entire winter was broken down to five days in February. We knew there would be good stormy weather to shoot – there always is at this time of year. But to be able to go out to sea in it isn't always possible because, well, apart from anything else, it is fucking dangerous.'

But Smith was delighted just to have free rein with the equipment for a few days. He has worked with big production companies before and always been answerable to a producer or director. 'This time I had it on my own terms so I could shoot it the way I wanted to.' So he'd found himself scooting up to Dublin on a Monday morning to sign contracts which charged him with taking absurdly expensive equipment into the ocean and returning it safely. 'I was driving from Dublin with half a million quid's worth of gear,' he said, laughing nervously. Mickey was going to spend the day filming from the water and he had already positioned Willie and Kevin Smith at precise locations on the cliffs. His worry was that the cameras the boys were lugging across the fields and down the goats' trail would be too heavy. They were going to communicate by two-way radio and the last thing he wanted was that his first instruction should involve them tracking back up the side of the cliff.

Mickey stood at the petrol pumps talking through all this and laughing lightly every so often. He has this puckish way of making everything seem like a bit of a lark even though he takes his film and photographic work absolutely seriously.

At the pier in Doolin the tourist office was firmly shut. A sign advertising burgers and French fries had been blanched of colour by the salty winter air. The boys had the place to themselves. Steph Skajarowski showed up driving a black jeep with a Relentless logo. Steve Thomas, a chipper Welshman, had been recruited to drive one of the three jet-skis for the day.

The preparation for days like this is a tedious ritual that they have gone through a thousand times. They moseyed through the repetitive tasks of selecting boards from their vans, attaching fins with allen keys, securing the boards on to the rescue pads, and then pulling on their wetsuits, hoods and boots. There is no pleasant way of getting changed outdoors on a February morning. Tom Lowe stood in the shelter of the ticket office doorway. Fergal just got ready beside his jet-ski. Steph got changed by the passenger door of his jeep, talking with Steve about the Six Nations rugby match between Ireland and Wales which had taken place on Sunday. Andrew Cotton, the big wave surfer from Devon, showed up along with Al Mennie. All the while you could hear waves bashing in the distance and not much else.

Mickey produced a bag of baby's Liga from his pocket. 'Breakfast,' he announced with a laugh. 'Anyone have some water?'

Steve dragged the jet-ski trailer over to the slipway and when they were ready they hitched his jet-ski to the rear of the jeep, which began to reverse down towards the water. The slipway was deathly slippery and the ski is such a heavy piece of machinery that it began to drag the jeep down the slope even after Fergal hit the brakes. They inched towards the water, and eventually Steph and Steve used a rope to winch the machine into the shallows until it was safe to unfasten the band holding the jet-ski in place and let it slip into the water. Then Steph jumped into waist-deep water and held the ski while the others went through the same process with the next two skis. It took about twenty minutes just to get all three jet-skis in the water. 'Beats going to the office anyhow,' Fergal said cheerfully at one point, skidding down the slope in his boots after he had parked the jeep up for the day. Mickey made his way more gingerly as he was carrying the camera he would be using for the day, moving carefully across the rocks until he was able to jump on to the ski. Then Steph hopped on behind him and held the camera.

Fergal drove with Tom Lowe as passenger, and Steve and Steph drove together. They headed out through the rough surf in tandem and bombed across the open plain of water in about ten minutes, navigating around the bigger breaks that rolled into their path and sweeping around in the deep water where Aileen's begins to form. Then Fergal, Tom and Steve untied the boards and slipped into the water while the others steered the jet-skis over to the left.

It was about ten o'clock in the morning, and they lay on their boards. The sea was choppy and the wave breaks infrequent. When the break levelled off it was hard to spot the surfers from the cliff top: they were just shadows on the water. The wind was cold and constant and there were few people at Moher. Even the visitors' centre up the road was quiet. Yanni came along to film the surfing for the morning and found a hollow from where she could train the camera on the wave breaks. It was a Tuesday morning, and the world was quiet.

Mickey spent eight hours in the water, too involved in shooting his film to follow how the surfing was going. He wanted the film he took to be at water level so he slid off the ski into the water, kicking his legs for buoyancy and balancing the camera on his shoulder. He has learned how to do this down the years, using his shoulder like a tripod while he kicks his legs like crazy. The problem was the batteries on the camera only lasted for half an hour and then he had to go back to shore to reload it with a spare. That meant skiing in until the surf began to crash against the rocks and then half swimming, half body-surfing in with the tide, cradling the camera with his shoulder whenever he bashed against a rock.

'The swell was south and the low tides were huge, so it was

tricky. Going in was all right – you could kind of float in. But getting back out, you have to run across these slippery boulders and get into the water before the wave smashes. And you have this sixty grand camera in your hand . . . I don't think they would let you do that if there was a producer there. They'd just close it down. But you know, I returned it to them without a scratch on it. So the rest of the week I had it better organized. That dealing with the batteries thing was just stupid. My landlord has a big boat and we rented that for the week. Steve drove and Willie was out on the boat as well. I was just trying to capture as many landscapes from the sea [as I could] – waves smashing into the cliffs, and just getting as close as I could to them. It is hard to do. You just keep getting bashed up. We had all sorts of calamities going on that week. Like with Ferg's Land Rover.'

The next morning they wanted to shoot film under Hag's Head so they decided to launch the boat they had acquired from the pier at Liscannor. They went through the same rigmarole: rising at dawn and packing all the equipment, checking the tide, filling the jet-skis with petrol, peeling damp wetsuits over their limbs in the salty morning air, and then figuring out the best way of getting themselves seaborne. They have had several misadventures down the years trying to launch jet-skis; Mickey Smith looks upon their first few months as a miracle that nobody got squashed to death. The difficulty on this particular morning was how to navigate the stretch of mud flats that divided the end of the pier from the beginning of the tide.

After careful deliberation they decided that the wisest thing to do would be simply to drive through it. 'Really fast,' Mickey laughs. 'It was typical us. We just told ourselves it would work out.' So Fergal revved the engine up on the slope of the pier, the boat hitched to the rear of the Land Rover. Mickey, Tom, Steve and Steph stood at the harbour, arms folded, looking authoritative. Fergal floored it and everything went perfectly for about fifteen metres, but then the jeep just disappeared as if it had hit quicksand. Everything below the bonnet was gone. For a few moments nobody spoke, then everyone started coming up with various suggestions. 'All of us trying to pretend that we have all these man-skills to cope with situations like this,' Mickey says. 'When we haven't got any.'

They could hear Fergal shouting from the cabin of the jeep. 'Ehhh, boys? Think I'm a bit stuck here.'

They kept their calm. First they tried to dig the mud away from the rear tyres with a shovel. Nothing budged. Then someone decided to let the air out of the tyres. It made no impression on the jeep, which felt as if it had been set in cement. The group was perspiring, caked in mud, and clueless as to what to do next.

Someone heard a tractor in the distance and Steph ran up and more or less begged the driver to help. Obligingly, the farmer took a detour to the pier and scratched his head at the sight of this gorgeous black Land Rover (it sports the Relentless logo on its side in Gothic font) marooned in the mud. He noticed, as they all did, that the tide was on its way in, and fast. Fergal was still in the driver's seat, his head peering out the window.

By now, word of an interesting diversion at the pier had begun to spread through Liscannor and fishermen were standing at the top of the pier watching. Some of them were taking pictures with their phones so they would have proof later on when they told friends and family about the monumental stupidity they were witnessing. It wasn't every day that you got to see an expensive Land Rover getting swallowed up by the sea, but by eleven o'clock the tide would do just that. Some members of the audience called out with occasional helpful observations, such as 'Yez are fucked, boys'. Fergal, whose fuse wouldn't be the longest, asked them if they wanted to come down and help, but they said no.

This was Mickey's worst nightmare. He has always felt self-conscious about how frivolous surfing must look to outsiders, with its equipment and surf wear. They rarely used the pier at Liscannor and weren't well known there. In Doolin they have come to know the fishermen and have occasionally obliged them by retrieving fishing pots washed under the cliffs. They show up in the wildest of weather, winter and summer, and go about their business quietly. They have arrived back at the pier on jet-skis ferrying injured surfers; once, they had to deal with someone with a broken back. And they didn't panic: they knew what they were at. In Doolin they had earned their stripes. But they were virtual strangers at Liscannor, and Mickey Smith knew how this looked. 'This flash jeep with crazy writing all over it and jet-skis . . . I imagine it seemed like a bunch of toys to them. They have their boats and they are hard-working men. They probably think we are just flashy pricks. Rich kids, or whatever. Normally the pier would be empty on a winter's morning but it's been such a mild winter that I suppose there are more people about. So they were on their phones: look at these fucken eejits. Couldn't blame 'em.'

But this one farmer kept on trying to pull their jeep out.

They used his supply of ropes, which immediately snapped. Then they broke a chain. Then they snapped a bigger chain. All the time Fergal offered a commentary from the driver's seat. By now he could see the water approaching the bonnet. He peered through the windscreen grimly, like Captain Smith on the *Titanic*. 'We're sinking, boys. Startin' to go down here.'

The rescue party were out of ideas when one of the fishermen called from above. They looked up to see an elderly man complete with a white beard straight from the fables in the process of lobbing something down to them. It was the biggest rope any of them had ever seen, as thick as a tree trunk.

'What the fuck we meant to do with this?' Steph screamed.

'Tie it through the windows,' the old man advised. 'It's your last chance.'

They discussed it and were convinced that rather than dislodge the jeep it would just rip the top of it clean off. 'Doesn't matter anyway,' Mickey consoled Fergal. 'It's going to drown in a minute.'

So they rolled down the windows and ran the rope through the interior of the jeep. By the time the farmer had secured the rope to his tractor the water was lapping against the bonnet. The tractor strained and roared and the crowd was fascinated and then to everyone's disbelief the jeep sort of jumped free from the mud. The tractor then succeeded in hauling it back to dry land.

The next few seconds were filled with bedlam. The farmer, who had been stoical in his labours for a full half hour, was delighted with his success. He jumped out of the cab of his tractor, gave the fingers to the gathering on the pier and shouted in triumph, 'Now fuck off!' The boys were howling for joy. Fergal shook his fist through the window of the jeep. Mickey simply ran up to the old man who had thrown down the enormous rope and wrapped him in a hug. 'I think he was offended,' Smith says ruefully. 'He looked at me like I had committed this cardinal sin and walked away. Some bloke in a wetsuit hugging him! I was thinking: he was just trying to help and this is how I repay him. But I was just so happy.'

Five minutes later it was back to business. Fergal parked the Land Rover up. It had become a daft two-tone: pristine from the bonnet up, caked in mud from the door handles down. They made short work of launching two jet-skis, Mickey swam out to where the boat was with his camera, and within minutes the group was tearing off into the surf.

Smith spent another full day out on the water, this time from the relative luxury of the boat. He knew in his heart that he had more than enough footage and that only a handful of seconds might be included in the final edit of the film. But he has never been practical or commercial about film and, again, a combination of instinct and fascination with the landscape and the sheer joy of having these cameras all to himself took over. Willie was at the bottom of the cliffs, having spent the morning lugging equipment down the hazardous goats' trail. They chatted away on walkie-talkie so they could capture the same sequence of water hitting rocks from different angles. It might contribute only a second or two to the film but he wanted them to be memorable. Fergal and Tom spent the day surfing but it was one of those days that tested patience: rarely did the wave break cleanly enough for either of them.

The sky was dusky by the time they returned to Liscannor and the lights in the village looked cheerful. It was full tide, and as they pulled into the pier somebody pointed out that they were right over the spot where the Land Rover could, perhaps should, have been. When they cut the motor, all you could hear was laughter.

The feature film hit the cinemas in early summer. It represented yet another way in which the Cliffs of Moher and the ocean crashing against it have featured, obliquely or otherwise, on television and film down the decades.

In 2003 a new advert from Guinness appeared on Irish television. It depicted a man walking across Ireland, swimming the Atlantic and then showing up sodden in a New York shebeen. It was another dazzling burst of commercial creativity. In a matter of seconds the rugged hero strode across the midland plains and the Burren, swam hard into a vast green ocean, and was under Liberty's steadfast gaze just a few strokes later; he barged through a game of pick-up basketball on an asphalt court in Manhattan, past the Naked Cowboy in Times Square, and cut a determined path through a definitively Village street with the usual siren sounds and hubbub in the background before entering the pub, seeking out a friend of his and uttering the word 'Sorry'. The advert was entitled 'Quarrel' and helped to make a hit of the accompanying song 'Heyday' for the late Mic Christopher, as well as showcasing a young Kerry actor named Michael Fassbender to a wider audience. It was broadcast when the country felt molten with economic success and the Atlantic divide between America and Ireland had never felt less significant: it was around that time that stories began to emerge of the affluent Irish day-tripping to New York for shopping or, even more preposterously, for lunch. The idea of some guy swimming the pond for a conciliatory pint of stout with a friend was no big deal.

But the most visually arresting sequence in the advert disturbed some viewers. The hero chooses the Cliffs of Moher as his diving board, and for a breathtaking few seconds he is filmed standing on the very edge looking down at the white water crashing below him. In the next scene he is executing a perfect dive filmed from under the water. The Clare county coroner, Isobel O'Dea, was not alone in seeing the images as potentially upsetting for families who had lost loved ones through accidents or suicide at the Cliffs of Moher. Newspaper reports chronicled the efforts of a Clare-based Garda superintendent named Sean Corcoran to express his reservations about the advert. He had written to both RTÉ and Guinness explaining exactly why he found the commercial so troubling. 'The Cliffs of Moher are known not only for their beauty but also, unfortunately, as a place where an untold number of suicides have been committed,' read the letter as quoted in the *Irish Independent*. 'Your advert is callous, insensitive, and downright offensive to the parents and families of many people who have unfortunately committed suicide at the Cliffs. These people come not only from Clare but all over Ireland.'

The misgivings were acknowledged, but at RTÉ the feeling was that the storyline of the commercial was so fabulously escapist that viewers would not make the connection between it and the personal tragedies. Over time the advert was forgotten, but the controversy shone a light on the darker aspect of the Cliffs of Moher. It illustrated the fact that the cliffs will always be a kaleidoscopic place, beautiful and sombre and sacred. O'Brien's tower stands as testimony to that fact, having attracted sightseers since at least as far back as the 1850s. But alongside the thousands of people who have stood upon the cliffs and marvelled there are many others for whom the place is associated with heartbreak and despair.

The waters are dangerous in all kinds of ways. In 1915, a report in the *New York Times* carried the headline 'Vanderbilt's Body Not Recovered'. 'A body which was believed to be that of Alfred G. Vanderbilt who was lost in the *Lusitania* disaster was washed ashore on Wednesday night on the Clare coast at Doolin, near the Cliffs of Moher,' the first paragraph read. 'Yesterday however the police authorities satisfied themselves that the body was not that of Mr Vanderbilt although it appeared to tally with the published description and a gold watch found on its clothing bore initials corresponding to that of Mr Vanderbilt.' So members of the Vanderbilts, one of America's most illustrious families, had walked the Irish coastline in the months after the *Lusitania* was torpedoed by a German submarine but never found their son.

Every decade has had its tragedies. In August 1983, a group of young people attending the Lisdoonvarna music festival went swimming off Trá Lathàin in Doolin close to the Cliffs of Moher. Eight men were drowned in one of the worst swimming disasters in the history of the state. They were caught in waters that weren't particularly deep but the rip tides and currents are notorious. As Noel Carmody of the Clare Civil Defence explained at the time, the swimmers were dealing with three distinct currents: one from the sea, one from Inishmaan and one from the Cliffs of Moher. The combination could pull all sorts of strange tricks in the area around Trá Latháin. For years afterwards the legacy of the tragedy was the most potent way of reminding casual swimmers of just how dangerous the local waters could be.

One of the most poignant stories concerned a lady who had spent most of her life away from Ireland working with a religious order in Spain before spending two decades as a housekeeper in Boston until her death in 1967. Her abiding wish was to be buried in her native Inishmaan. On a day of strong winds, a helicopter carrying the lady's remains in a coffin secured by a freight sling took off from Lahinch golf course. Just fifteen minutes later the sling somehow became loose and the coffin fell into the sea. A search was conducted about two miles off Hag's Head in a line with Inishmaan but despite an extensive operation the coffin was never found. The stretch of water was as close to home as she got. It must be one of the very saddest stories of Irish emigration, a topic about which many thick volumes have been written.

The cliffs have acquired a mythological status. Just about every travel article ever written about Ireland has contained a reference to them and they feature on the itineraries of all tourist bus tours roaming the west of Ireland. Visiting celebrities and dignitaries are frequently photographed standing at the cliffs looking (as everyone does) slightly un-nerved by the sheer drop and the panorama on offer. The Beatles visited there; the ashes of Dusty Springfield were scattered over the cliffs; in February 2012 the Chinese Vice President Xi Jinping was taken there during his barnstorming tour of Ireland, and encountered a lone protester, a woman by the name of Sinéad Ní Ghairbith who wore a placard reading

'Free Tibet'. Late last year Michael Flatley's plans to stage an extravagant concert at the Cliffs of Moher fell apart.

When David Lean came to Kerry to film *Ryan's Daughter* in 1969, he couldn't resist using the cliffs in his opening scene, in which a gust of wind swipes the bonnet Sarah Miles is wearing as she walks along the headland. Two years later John Huston had more spectacular action in mind, using Doolin and the narrow roads up to the cliffs as the backdrop for a car chase in *The Mackintosh Man*. Paul Newman drives a beat-up Ford Transit with Dominique Sanda sitting demurely by his side and a white Mercedes in hot pursuit, and nary a Garda patrol car in sight. One coolly executed 360-degree turn and the loss of traction on a gravelly road leads to the whole point of the scene: the expensive Mercedes busting through a stone wall, rolling down the flat stone platforms at the top of the cliffs, and then crashing into the sea below. Tom Cruise and Nicole Kidman filmed at the cliffs during their madcap historical caper *Far and Away*.

And it was to the cliffs that Rob Reiner headed when he was making *The Princess Bride*, the 1987 film of William Goldman's cult fantasy classic. The film starred Robin Wright, and Moher was used as the Cliffs of Insanity. In one of the most spectacular scenes, Andre the Giant is seen shimmying up the face of the cliffs with the irate Wallace Shawn and Wright as the fair damsel hanging on to him.

So it is a place with many faces and decades of energy. Its new role as the backdrop to a splendid wave is just the latest – something of which the surfers who swim in its shadow are implicitly aware. Even when Mickey Smith first saw Aileen's he understood that he wasn't really laying claim to it. Nobody can 'own' a wave. It was there for millions of years before he laid eyes on it and it is anyone's guess how many millions of years it has ahead of it. Even on sunny days when they have the wave to themselves the place has an aura. They all understood that decades before they began to surf there the Cliffs of Moher was a forbidding beauty spot that, more than anything, made visitors feel minute and insignificant. And they knew the cliffs as a place of unspeakable sadness and poignancy as well. You can't spend time there without at least fleetingly thinking of those who have fallen over the years, having lost their footing, or having been pushed by the sudden gusts of wind that occur there, or having stepped off while in the grip of unimaginable despair. Like the Golden Gate Bridge in San Francisco, the Cliffs of Moher have become established down the years as a place where people come to end their lives. Every so often cars are found abandoned there and the newspapers carry stark reports of a body found. Most of the surfers who live in the area have been involved in the hasty searches organized in the days afterwards.

'The Cliffs of Moher, for me . . . I have never been attracted to the place, I don't like it,' Bill Keane admitted one day. 'There is a resonance to that place that you don't find anywhere else. An awful lot of people have gone up there to jump off so it is very powerful. You go up there and you just get a sense of energy up there and you think: what the fuck is going on here? I think if you asked a lot of people in Clare, they would say they wouldn't go up there much. When the sun shines and there is no wind, it is gorgeous, yes. But when the wind is howling, it is different. The thing is, I do a lot of fishing from the bottom of the cliffs. And it is way more beautiful from below looking up than it is from the top looking down. And it is a much safer and nicer place to be, down at the Atlantic looking up. I don't know, it's because you feel as if you are a part of it from down there. But when I am at the top I get a completely different feeling. It's strange.'

When the Clare lads began surfing there and the wave started to generate international publicity, they were all worried about what would happen if less experienced surfers showed up, youngsters who just fancied taking it on. What if there was a fatality? 'That is something you think about,' Mickey Smith says. 'But after a while we learned that the wave kind of sorts itself out. People may turn up there with the intention of surfing it but once you are at the bottom of the cliffs and you can see what the wave is about, you quickly realize if you are up to it or not.'

Sometimes Fergal will look up from his board and see a crowd gathered on the cliff and become uneasy. He has been up there when strong gusts of wind suddenly whip up from nowhere. The old Clare County Council signs warn about landfalls, too. 'The place is no secret any more and it is a bit frightening to think that people come there to watch us, because anyone could easily fall off there. It does make you feel a bit responsible in some way.'

It is an admirable concern, and understandable. But the truth is that even if Aileen's had never been surfed, people would have found reasons to walk that headland. In 2007, the new visitors' centre was opened. Plans for the centre had first been drafted some seventeen years earlier, and through objections to and arguments over the merits of the idea they had changed considerably. The final result was in keeping with the heady, fast-spending attitude of the time. The project cost €31.5 million and its aspiration was to merge the natural moodiness and power of the cliffs with the comfort and convenience of sparkling tourist amenities. The place became known as the Cliffs of Moher Experience, much as the whirling dervish guitar solos of Jimi Hendrix were sanitized over time. The new centre, glass-fronted and cut into the hill, looks impressive. There is ample space for the coach operators who ferry tourist groups there every day. Shops featuring souvenirs and local crafts and playing traditional music break the tedium of the walk to the restaurant and the interpretative centre. The restaurant is tasteful and comfortable and every kind of gift imaginable has been stamped with the Moher logo. The interpretative centre explores the geological and mythological history of the cliffs; one of its most crowd-pleasing items features the cliffs as seen through the eyes of a diving gannet. As a project it advertised the fact that Ireland was anything but a half-baked tourism backwater.

'Ocean, rock, nature, man – a giant cathedral on our western shore' was the description of Moher used by Bertie Ahern, the Taoiseach of the day, in his opening address. And that is exactly what it is. An estimated one million visitors had stood at the heights the previous year, making it easily the most magnetic tourist attraction in Ireland, much as visitors on once-in-a-lifetime trips to California gravitate towards the Grand Canyon. The metamorphosis of the cliffs was in keeping with governmental plans to aggressively push Ireland as a first port of call for international tourists. Now, the most famous patch of land in Ireland had become part of the package. 'We could only put it in place because of the fact that we have built the economy to the point where we were able to build up our tourism product and we aim to spend 317 million euros in the life of the next government,' vowed John O'Donoghue, the Minister for Tourism, at the opening of the centre. 'Our ambition for the tourism industry knows no bounds. By the end of 2012 we will increase the number of visitors to this country by ten million.'

This was the mood then: bullish, confident. The pristine new centre was a manifestation of a rampantly ambitious government giddy with the possibilities created by a seemingly endless source of revenue.

There were reservations, of course. Not everyone was happy with the development. Coach operators were less than enamoured with the new parking fees that went with the immaculate facilities. And the legion of buskers, the warbling tin whistlers and folkie guitar heroes who had for years used the cliffs as an ideal spot to serenade the public, learned that they would have to audition for the right to play there in future. And for some people the commercial imperative at the heart of the new centre felt as wrong as putting a bridle on a wild horse.

The presence of the shops and the carefully designed centre seemed to compromise the very reason why people wanted to go and stand at the cliffs and gaze out on to the ocean. Moher is not a conventional beauty spot in the way that the Lakes of Killarney are. Moher is confrontational in its starkness and wildness and otherworldliness. It is unsettling. For anyone walking there for the first time it must seem as if they have in some way reached the very end of the earth. Bill Keane is right. It is a disturbing place. So the idea that visitors could now step up and expose themselves to the lonely majesty of the place before racing into the café for a comforting cappuccino – and buy the mug afterwards – felt to some people like the Disneyfication of something elemental.

But maybe the Cliffs of Moher Experience is just a progression, the twenty-first-century response to the fancy viewing tower Corny O'Brien built during the Famine from where, on days when the sea is boisterous, you can just about make out the shadows of surfers moving through the water.

8

Keskerdh Kernow

Mickey Smith's *Dark Side of the Lens* appeared on Vimeo in 2010. It is both a powerful ode to the Atlantic seascape and a quietly spoken manifesto for how he wants to live his life. It has attracted millions of views, and even allowing for the peculiar nakedness with which people post their opinions online, the praise this six-minute film draws is evangelical.

Smith made the film at the Cliffs of Moher, and from the opening seconds it draws people into the bewitchery of the place. From the first frames, where snow-white water bashes against the rocks, cascades from the stacks with a low hiss, detonates from the caves and comes gushing through the sea-cut arches and hollows tucked underneath the cliffs – all in a slowed-down motion which emphasizes that this place is somehow beyond mankind (Smith is then seen walking across a headland of mist-shrouded cliffs) – the film has a hypnotic quality which plunges its audience into this elsewhere of cold water and metallic sky.

'Life on the road is something I was raised to embrace,' come the opening words. And then a silhouette in the shiny seal skin of a wetsuit tumbles off a rock ledge into the water, and for the next five minutes the Cliffs of Moher are presented as never before: through barrelling waves and lush foam; as a magnificent backdrop for soaring dolphins; through the caverns that run beneath its sea face; from the heart of the emerald green power of Aileen's; and on those wet, misty days when the tourists stay away from the cliffs which are, in fact, the very days that frame the place as it should be seen, druidic and untameable. Smith states his intention in one frame of film when a dropping sun is captured through the tiny circle in a concrete stake through which a coil of barbed wire runs: he just wants to take snapshots of those 'subtle glimpses of magic other folk might pass by'.

From the outset Smith lays himself bare, showcasing to the world what seems like a wonderful secret. The film and its accompanying message are unabashedly open, but even though the film was made for public consumption it was, in essence, a private letter to his sister.

'Cherry. She died in 2010. Her heart stopped,' Mickey explained one afternoon in his house. It was springtime, and it was the first time his life had slowed down in months. He and Riv had one day at home before they were setting off again. Just the previous week he had been working on the videos he made and produced for Ben Howard, the folk musician from Devon. He had spent days and nights in the studio, working to a precise schedule: a first cut Monday, a second Tuesday, a final cut on Wednesday, grade it and send it off on Thursday. Now he, Riv and Eiva were heading to England to shoot some film of Howard on a tour. That meant at least three weeks out of the country. Smith couldn't remember when he had ever had such a crammed workload, and even though he seemed tired as he sat drinking tea, he also felt blessed. And he sometimes thinks that any good fortune he has had can be traced back to the short film he made for his sister.

'She was twenty-six,' he continued quietly. 'She had two little boys – my nephews. And she was always so supportive of what I do. She would say to me: I love seeing the stuff that you do of everyone else out there on the water but I want to know what you do in the water. So when she died I decided I would make that film for her. There, that's her.' He pointed at a photograph on the wall. It was a close-up of a younger Smith wearing Docs and shorts and mugging for the camera as he stands beside a pretty girl who is laughing at his antics. They are little more than kids and are the picture of health. 'She was like my best mate. She wasn't a surfer at all. She was a crazy Goth. That was at the Reading festival a few years back. So it's been a fucked-up couple of years.'

Cherry and Mickey Smith were born and bred in Penzance. It was a magical place for a youngster; all you needed to know was that you were in the heart of pirate country and imagination did the rest. Who knew what shipwrecks were out there, or how many treasure chests had been dragged up the beach and into the caves and tunnels that are commonplace all along the coast? Most of the pubs in the area have tunnels running directly down to coves, and Prussia Cove, where they hung out as children, has a series of tunnels that lead directly up to the church. Penzance has a rich pull in terms of exotic history, fishing traditions, and the artisan shops and restaurants that flourish each summer when tourists arrive in search of West Country authenticity. And for twelve months of the year it also has the sea.

When Mickey thinks back to when he really began to understand how important the sea was to him, he places himself on the local beach when he was about eight years old. 'That is when I remember surfing every day. Where we grew up is on a peninsula and there were beaches all around us. My mum and dad had split up and got divorced properly and Mum took us to the beach every single day that summer. And I was just buzzing to be out there all day on this piece of foam. The same people used to go there, so we made friends with other kids. A lot of the waves break right on the sand in a big hollow and are just great fun for bodyboarding. And the heavy waves that I like now are that shape.'

Anyone who grows up in Cornwall becomes conscious of the separateness of the place. You breathe it in along with the salt air. They had all learned about the Cornish rebellion in school, when thousands of Cornishmen marched all the way to London in protest at the taxes imposed by Henry VII, only to be summarily eviscerated by the Crown's forces. But that incident, in June 1497, was simply the most overt manifestation of a restlessness that comes with being Cornish. It didn't matter whether you were a blacksmith like Michael An Gof, who spearheaded that doomed revolt, or any of the myriad surfers who were kicking around the coastal towns in the 1990s when Smith and his friends were growing up there. Cornwall just feels apart, tucked down in the southernmost corner of England, spiritually disconnected from the road to London by the river Tamar, by the remnants of its Cornish language, by the flag which hangs on most guesthouses, and by its superstitions and festivals and the natural affinity of its people for the Celtic tradition. Simply by turning to face the sea, generations of Cornish people turned their back on Olde England and on everything that entailed.

For centuries, to young Cornishmen the sea meant toil and fishing – a livelihood. For Mickey Smith, the sea meant escape and self-expression through endless hours spent bodyboarding and surfing with Steph Skajarowski, one of his oldest friends. Steph had first seen Smith one evening playing his drum kit with a punk band he was in. 'Mickey can't have been any more than eleven,' Steph laughs. It was a sight he remembered. Then they met up on the beach shortly after that and became fast friends. 'What I remember most is getting to the beach in winter pre-light, spending the entire day there and then getting picked up after dark,' Steph adds. 'We were always terrified of missing something, so we waited until it was dark. So we seemed to spend a lot of time absolutely freezing on the shore and mucking around in the dark waiting for the parents to turn up.'

The sea was their playground, but they always understood its potency. Fishermen go back through the generations in Mickey Smith's family. His grandfather, who ran the coast-guard station for West Penwith, had to deal with tragedies periodically and had the harrowing task of visiting the families of those bereaved by the Penlee lifeboat disaster, one of the most evocative maritime tragedies of recent decades. At around tea-time on 19 December 1981 the engines failed on a coaster cargo vessel carrying eight people including the captain's wife and two stepdaughters. After attempts to winch the passengers into a Navy helicopter failed, the shout went out to launch the lifeboat. Eight volunteers headed out on the *Solomon Browne*, which launched from Mousehole, a village stacked on the coastline with its pier walls slanting outwards as if to cradle the place from the ocean. This was after eight o'clock on the last Saturday before Christmas under pitch-black skies and into the wildest of seas: sixty-foot waves and hurricane-force winds. Through a valorous feat of seamanship – at one stage a ferocious wave actually pitched the lifeboat on to the deck of the cargo vessel – the *Solomon Browne* crew managed to get four of those on the stricken vessel on board: the crew watching from the helicopter above could just about make out their fluorescent jackets crossing the deck and jumping into the waiting arms of the lifeboat crew. They had just radioed their intention to rescue the remaining crew when the communication was abruptly replaced by a silence of chilling finality. Both boats foundered on the rocks off the coast; all sixteen lives were lost. Funerals were held on Christmas Eve and again on Boxing Day.

'He had seen some terrible disasters down the years but after that he had to go around and see all the families because he was in charge,' Mickey Smith says of his grandfather. 'They were his men. My mum says he was never the same afterwards.'

In the year of the twenty-fifth anniversary of the disaster Steph was working in a local hotel for the summer when a film crew from the BBC came to make a documentary. 'We were all good friends with the receptionist there. Her husband had been one of the crew on the lifeboat. She never spoke about it much but whenever you hear about it now it just seems nothing short of a tragedy. For something like that to happen in a small community isn't something that will ever be forgotten. And it is always going to make you have a lot of respect for the sea as well.'

They were just about old enough to witness the rapid deterioration of traditional economic certainties. Too many of the small fishing ports around Newlyn were reduced to ghostyards. The tin mines began to close in the 1970s, and the fishing boats went out in ever fewer numbers. And all along the coast beautiful houses were shuttered all winter and peopled by strangers in the summer. They were on open fields but the signs warning trespassers were clear. So even when they were children, the penny began to drop. 'You soak all that up,' Smith says. 'Being Cornish is the strangest sense of identity because you feel as if you have nothing to do with England in terms of cities like London or wherever. But then Cornwall is more or less owned by the royal family. It's a duchy. So it is hard being a kid there because you see all the riches around you, but it's private land and it belongs to people who have second or third homes there. The land is out of bounds. Very few people in Cornwall own anything of substance like that.'

For visitors, walking through towns and villages like St Ives, Penzance and Mousehole was and remains magical, like stepping into a dreamy painting by Turner. But the summer season is a veneer. The restaurants, craft shops and quaint coffee shops with their local produce are real enough and wonderful but there is another side that the visitors don't see.

Wander far enough off the cobbled streets, beyond the light the restored gas lamps throw and away from the harbour at that time when the sun is dipping, the lights are twinkling and the town feels heavenly – an idyll, as the brochures say – and you will find areas of squalor and poverty that can match the grimmest of England's failed industrial cities of the north. In recent decades families have been moved wholesale to Cornwall from troubled estates in far-away cities in the hope that this strange place with its bracing air will help them turn things around. Instead, social problems are being packed up along with clothes and saucepans. 'Proper little gangs,' Mickey says with a dark laugh. 'Cornwall's one of the poorest parts of Britain now, I think. The level of education and the delinquency is quite shocking. It is fucking heavy in places now. A lot of drugs come through Cornwall and that brings nasty characters in as well. Thankfully there is still a bit of a community vibe in west Cornwall. But it's a sad history really.'

Still, this was the land they inherited when they came into the world and they made of it what they could. When Smith was nine he went on his first trip to London, with his school football team. His mum gave him a disposable camera to take snaps of Trafalgar Square or Buckingham Palace or any of the sights they might pass. 'We were in a hotel room, which was a huge deal for us. There were teachers around but we were on our own. And I took a photo from that hotel window of the sunset. I think I still have that photo somewhere.'

That simple snapshot of London at sundown was the beginning. In the summers after that his mum bought him waterproof cameras, and so began his first attempts at photographing the ocean and sea life. Sometimes the film contained thirty-five frames; sometimes it came with two extra bonus frames. But he could make them last for months because he was so choosy about when he pressed snap. 'Just spent all day looking for any cool stuff worth filming. I guess that is where all this comes from.'

Steph remembers how thrifty Smith could be with those shots. 'The days of thirty-five millimetre! He would swim out and have thirty-five shots and that was it. He had to make them count. But even then the composure of the shots and the timing he had was brilliant. It probably seems as if Mickey could turn his hand to whatever he felt like but that is how it was.'

As far as the others were concerned, Smith was a force of nature. By his teens he was known locally as a bodyboarder who stalked the heaviest waves in the locality. And he had this nocturnal life as a musician, hurling himself into performances with the same abandon and energy with which he approached surfing. Last autumn Smith was invited to give a talk at the Do Lectures in Wales, where he elaborated on how important music was to him. He told the audience of learning to play drums and guitar as a youngster and of heading out on the road for gigs. He was easily the youngest member of the band, sometimes wriggling in on top of the amps and other gear when the van was full, stretching out and listening to whatever was playing on the tape deck. They played everything from working men's clubs and gatherings for the British Legion to rarefied hotel ballrooms where tourists sipped drinks and half listened. He began to treat those gigs as brilliant learning experiences because he was being exposed to every level of society. 'After-hours life education' was his quaint description of those touring years at the Do Lectures, where his theme was to encourage people to follow whatever interest or passion in life they hold dearly.

Music and nature became his twin fascinations. It was as a musician that most of his friends first saw him. 'He was always playing in these punk bands in St Ives and I would go see them,' says Tom Lowe. 'I was way too young to be allowed in but I would blag a way into some club and you'd see the biggest mosh pit you could ever imagine. There are some nutters in St Ives. Real hard men who surfed hard as well. So Mickey was there hammering away in these Gothic metal bands when he was a kid. It was hilarious, thinking back. Thing is, he's a serious musician. He would never say it. We might be in the van in Clare and he will stick something on and we will be chatting and then you'd ask him if that was him. And it would be fucking brilliant. But it's hard to even get him to pick up the guitar in the house if there are people around. Anyway, I would meet Mickey at parties a few times then. We were all living real fast and he was flying about the place. He would be there, partying hard as he did then, and just be super friendly. It doesn't matter who he is speaking with, he gives one hundred per cent concentration. But I wasn't too sure of myself around him. I remember he said something good about my surfing once and I just kind of clammed up and walked away. Wasn't sure what to say to him.'

But Smith, through his love for music and the sea, began to formulate a future that was not necessarily defined by the socio-economic realities of west Cornwall. He began to understand that he didn't have to accept the order of things as they were handed down to him, that with the encouragement of his mother and his sister he could just follow his own path.

By his mid-teens most of the young surfers he knew were itching to go on the road. It was a rite of passage. Older Cornish surfers would return tanned and dreamy-eyed after spending winters in exotic places. They traded mundane months working menial jobs at home just to get enough money together to escape. Then they came home and started saving again. For anyone with a bit of adventure in their souls it seemed like a good life.

Tom Lowe set off on his own path. Although he had never spoken about it with Smith, he shared with him a conflicted attitude towards Cornwall: he was fiercely passionate but disenchanted about the way it was going and the life it promised. 'Here in Clare you can trust your kids on the street, although it does feel that there are more people about now and there are types about that aren't as good-natured and that maybe the vibe is changing. But in Newquay you would be having a lovely night out and just get beaten up. Guys want trouble and Jesus, they will give it to you. They are just pissed up. It doesn't matter if you are a surfer or whatever.'

Through surfing, they left the aggravation behind.

Mickey and Steph began with little trips to the Canaries, but as soon as school was done they bolted for the southern hemisphere. By then Mickey was so absorbed in photography that he spent as much time documenting as he did bodyboarding. He had learned how to develop his own film, and then when digital photography began to replace film he taught himself how to use that. He used money he had earned from playing in the band to buy a camera and housing for underwater shots but always remained faithful to his belief that the equipment was just a variation on those disposable cameras he had used as a boy. They were just little machines, beautiful and simple.

He spent a couple of years serving out a private apprenticeship, getting better on his own terms. But in terms of commerce, he was useless. He was living in Western Australia at the age of nineteen and had spent a few days in the water filming local surfers as they went about their business, with no idea of what he might do with the material. This was around the time when he was so happy to blow with the wind that he actually spent a year making decisions based on the flip of a lucky coin he carried. In Western Australia he bumped into a few surf film makers who were well established at the time and who were putting together a documentary. He showed them the footage he had taken – three of them sitting on the settee in the cramped van which Smith called home – and was taken aback by their enthusiasm. They offered to pay him for the footage but he was so flattered by their interest that he just handed it over to them, gratis. They ended up using most of it. That same week he had taken some film of a local competition and passed it on to some guy from a television station who expressed an interest in it. The footage ended up on cable news that night and caused a local sensation. In the days afterwards people were coming up to him telling him they had seen his stuff. Naturally they presumed he was selling his material.

'Everyone thought I was coining it, but I was just a little

fucking pikey living in a van,' he laughs. 'The bodyboarders and surfers told me I had to stop just giving stuff away. So I had to change my head and learn how to even contemplate selling it. It felt like a weird decision. It has always been like that for me. I'm learning! But I am fucking thirty-two now so it is time for me.'

Even now he tussles with a constant internal conflict be-tween the early joy of photographing the sea and surfers for the sake of it and the huckstering aspect of releasing those images for commercial publication. That tussle is particularly true in relation to Riley's.

Although Smith's name will always be associated with the wave at the Cliffs of Moher, it is the ragged little corner near Doonbeg that seems to mean most to him. He happened upon the place in October 2007, out rambling one afternoon to try to cope with the anxiety he felt at the news that Cherry was going through grave complications with her pregnancy. He was half in a trance, nowhere near focused enough to conduct a proper search for waves, yet he somehow stumbled on this obscure jewel tucked underneath a jagged fantasy of a rock shelf. It was perfect, entirely hidden from view unless you stood on the very edge of the headland. Once again he had that precious fleeting feeling of having a piece of the earth all to himself, except this time, because his mind was locked into his sister's distress back home in Cornwall, he felt a kinship with the place that has never left him. Which is why he went on to name the wave after his nephew Riley, happily born in perfect health shortly afterwards. 'It's always felt like a sanctuary, and since my sister passed away the place has pretty much become sacred to me, the place I feel closest to her on earth,' he wrote in an essay published in *Carve* magazine (issue 130). In that piece he lays bare the distress he feels at the way Riley's has been slowly stripped of that elementary magic as more and more surfers show up there and photographers set up their tripods on the headland and line it up in their sightline: a moody backdrop for a glossy photograph. Smith feels complicit in what Riley's has inexorably become: just another brilliant surfing location for visitors to tick off.

For Smith, the place has always been a shrine, as if it had always been there just waiting for him to claim it. And if that feels fanciful, then how to explain why he happened upon it on that grim day in October? Or why that wave has lavished unimaginable gifts on him in the last five years – almond-shaped barrels from which you couldn't but take jaw-dropping photographs, and madly exhilarating periods when each wave seemed better than the last and when he and the lads didn't bother talking through English but through primal screams and when the place, for all its barrenness, had this perfect God-given serenity that made them feel, on afternoons when the sun warmed the stones, as if they were privileged. Smith spent untold hours taking photographs there and released the images sparingly. So for a while it was little more than a localized myth. Riley's was like a Masonic society: you had to have someone take you along. But that couldn't last. It was inevitable, once the first photographs of Riley's were seen, that people would become curious about the place.

For Smith, watching Fergal paddle into the wave in a way nobody else could emulate, watching Tom Lowe charging through it or Dan or Tom Gillespie surfing their best ever wave there, seeing the faces of visitors like Paul Morgan, or watching Ollie O'Flaherty or Hugo Galloway getting to know the wave by spending day after day there – all this made sense. It felt as if everyone served an apprenticeship and respected what the place gave them. But now he might turn up at Riley's and see unfamiliar number plates on jeeps and new faces already in the water and long-range camera lenses trained on the wave. The effect is to make the place feel as if it is just another theatre for flashy shots that will finish up in flashy magazines. And he can't help but think that if he had never released those first photographs, the surfers might have preserved it, kept its perfection intact.

'For me the problems have started since people began showing up with an attitude of rape and pillage,' he wrote in the *Carve* essay.

In many ways this is all an end result of my photographing this wave and publishing these images in the first place. Rape and pillage is so far away from my attitude and personal motivations, but it's true, to some extent I am the root cause of my own pain. The bottom line is that I love this place more than anyone else. No one would be down here if it wasn't for my sister, and I have always protected the vibe of the place, have never exploited the location, never focused attention solely on Riley's; never sold it out for a quick buck and always sought to project a positive low-key vibe around documenting the wave riding that's gone down out there over the years. I can't help but feel twinges of regret over the way things have panned out lately.

It is, of course, an impossible wish: he could not go down there week after week without capturing what he sees on film, any more than Fergal Smith or Tom Lowe could sit on the rocks and never surf. The dilemma for Smith will always be that his reason for taking photographs has not changed since he started out. It is one thing taking snapshots of the waves that fascinate him. Selling them on and watching them end up as part of the global production line of surfing iconography is another. 'I never had a reason for doing it other than I like it,' he says now. 'I like the challenge of getting better at it. But I simply love riding waves down at Riley's, almost more than anywhere else in the world. The photography has always come second down there. I searched the world for a wave like that and I feel blessed and fortunate that it is in our lives. And I'm delighted that people get to share in the magic of the place. I just hope that people can be mindful enough to want to respect it and preserve what the place has for future generations. Because it would be a shame if we lost that.' Talent has taken him to the stage where he can make a living from photography, and even though he considers this a blessing, it won't ever sit easy.

He has his own heroes from surfing culture and they are rarely the contemporary superstars or the smiling chiselled wave riders of yesteryear. He is suspicious of the surf industry and of the big companies it has spawned and reckons that the mythology of surfing has been doctored and shaped to create crowd-pleasing tidy narratives. So when he discovered Riley's and began to take the photographs, the fear was that he was setting in motion a chain of events that would see the place lose the very qualities that set it apart. It was the same fear that confronted Craig Peterson and Kevin Naughton when they took their photographs in Petacalco in the early 1970s: the fear that in surfing, paradise can only ever be lost.

Portraits exist of almost all of the celebrated faces of the last generation of Native American warriors with the striking exception of Crazy Horse, the Oglala Sioux who, despite achieving national fame and notoriety in his brief life, managed to avoid having his photograph taken. He believed that the camera had the power to capture the soul. It sometimes seems that Smith is so dedicated to photographing the waves around Clare that he is trying to do just that: capture the energy as well as the physical beauty of the water.

And maybe that's why the dreary commercial transaction of selling them on depresses him. He is sometimes bothered too that the glossy double XL spreads of the photographs he takes will come to be regarded as his chief motivation for being out there. Anyone making a living through surfing in Ireland has to deal with a similar contradiction. For most days of the year it is essentially a solitary and obscure pursuit, but when Mickey's photographs of winter sessions at Aileen's or Riley's appear they command an audience.

The published photographs are just a sideshow, a glamorous distortion of the day-to-day reality of his life. There have been weeks and months when the phone never rang with commissions to do flashy shoots and he was counting the pennies, but he was still blissfully happy to be out there shivering on the water, his knuckles raw and his head sore and the sea pounding down upon him.

So when he made *Dark Side of the Lens*, it was to celebrate that. He says in the film during a five-minute-long in-cantation:

'My heart bleeds Celtic blood and I am magnetized to familiar frontiers: raw, brutal, cold coastlines for the right wave riders to challenge. This is where my heart beats hardest. I try to pay tribute to that magic through photographs. Weathering the endless storms for rare glimpses of magic each winter is both a blessing and a curse I relish. I want to see wave riding documented the way I see it in my head and the way I feel it in the sea. It's a strange set of skills to begin to acquire, and it's only achievable through time spent riding waves. All sorts of waves on all sorts of crafts means more time learning out in the water. Floating in the sea amongst lumps of swell, you'll always learn something. It's been a lifelong wise old classroom teacher of sorts, and hopefully always will be. Buried beneath headlands, shaping the coast, mind-blowing images of empty waves burn away at me. Solid ocean swells powering through deep cold water. Heavy waves . . . waves with weight. They coax from comfortable routine, ignite the imagination, convey some divine spark, whisper possibilities, conjure the situations I thrive amongst and love to document. We all take knocks in the process: broken backs, drownings, near drownings, hypothermia, dislocations, fractures, frostbite, head wounds, stitches, concussions, broke my arm – and that's just the last couple of years. Still look forward to getting amongst it each winter though, cold creeping into your core, driving you mad, day after day mumbling to yourself as you hold position and wait for the next set to come. The dark side of the lens – an art form unto itself and us, silent workhorses of the surfing world. There's no sugary cliché. Most folk don't even know who we are, what we do or how we do it, let alone want to pay us for it. I never want to take this for granted, so I try to keep motivations simple, real, positive. If I only scrape a living, at least it's a living worth scraping. If there's no future in it, at least it's a present worth remembering. For fires of happiness or waves of gratitude . . . for everything that brought us to that point on earth at that moment in time to do something worth remembering with a photograph or a scar. I feel genuinely lucky to hand on heart say I love doing what I do. And I may never be a rich man but if I live long enough I'll certainly have a tale or two for the nephews. And I dig the thought of that.'

If that sounds very serious and earnest, that's because it is. It is what Mickey Smith believes and what he lives. He figured that some might hammer him for laying it on so solemn. He expected some of his friends to tear into him and make fun of him. 'I was totally surprised. I thought people were going to rip the piss out of me. And I'm sure they probably have done, when I'm not about. Can't believe Tom Gillespie hasn't had a crack at me.' He laughs, then falls serious. 'But I didn't really care what people thought. I just wanted to do it for my sister, and to be honest.'

The integrity shines through in the six minutes of film. It seems highly probable that some of the millions of hits for *Dark Side of the Lens* are repeat viewings: many of the comments admit to watching it repeatedly. The comments come from the five continents, and therein lies the magic of the film – the thought of this community of perfect strangers tuning in from air-conditioned offices, high-rise apartments in muggy cities or college dormitories, or while waiting in train stations, during times when they feel stalled in their own lives and ambitions, finding solace and inspiration in revisiting the startlingly clear and beautiful stretch of Irish coastline that Smith celebrates in his film. The reason the film strikes such a chord is that it cuts straight through the clutter and white noise of everyday life to the universal wish to make the most of whatever time one has. And it's not about leaping into frigid waters or getting bashed against coastal boulders day in, day out. 'If there was a message there,' Smith says, 'it was that people should realize they have more going on for themselves than they give themselves credit for. Everyone has their own stuff that they think is cool, and they should be buzzing on that and going after it.'

So now, in one of those quirks of fate, since *Dark Side of the Lens* was made public Mickey has never been as busy. Getting to work on a cinema feature would have been unimaginable a few years ago. He has had several offers to make music videos over the last couple of years and, half to his own surprise, has accepted some of them and even enjoyed the process: Smith's chaotic body clock responds well to the commercial imperative to deliver everything instantly and he thinks nothing of working through the night for several days in a row to deliver a cut on time.

'It is all a good learning experience. And if it means I get to keep doing what I love with the surfing stuff and can get other work that pays, all the better. As long as I get excited and it's a challenge creatively, I will just adapt. If I can keep living and having fun, then that is ideal. I would never take this for granted. I'd have no fear about labouring on a site or whatever. I've done that before and I'd do it again. I just feel lucky to be doing what I am doing.'

That's the thing: even for something as superficial as a music video, he can't help losing himself a little bit in the countryside. He spent many hours hauling a camera around the headland during the unseasonably warm early days of December 2010 and just about got enough footage before the entire country was seized by a Siberian Christmas. And when the video began to appear on MTV and other places it was another illustration of just what Mickey Smith's main influence on the Cliffs of Moher has been. In his surfing stills and film, the audience is so wrapped up in the subject or the movement of the water it is easy to think of the cliffs as a magnificent prop to the photo. The main effect is so obvious that it almost passes unnoticed. Smith's photographs give people a chance to look back at the Cliffs of Moher and admire their splendour. For once, they aren't what they appear to be when you are standing on the daunting summit: the very end of the civilized world. When you are standing on the cliffs it is their sheer height and wildness and the truly scary sight of the isolated coastline below that people remember. But through Smith's camera, rather than the sensory overload they provoke, the cliffs become the star attraction. They become the beginning of something.

If his photographs of the cliffs are slowly becoming his signature photographs in the busy world of surf photography, then it is accidental. But then much of what has happened to Mickey Smith has been accidental. He just followed his instinct wherever it took him, and of all the places in the world nowhere mirrors the magical appeal of Cornwall as closely as Clare. And Clare has the waves. Sometimes he thinks about the first winters he spent on the North Shore in Hawaii observing the weirdness of an ostensibly quiet place when the carnival of the world surfing tour visited. He sometimes wonders how he would feel if Lahinch was exposed to all that. The perpetual circle – the winning of competitions, the elbowing for the best shots to sell to the magazines, the crowds and the merchandising – used to madden him. 'Who has done this and that and the mad money involved. Crazy money. The thing about the money is that it ruins the kids. They can start competing and earning money at a young age and then that is what the whole thing becomes.' But it's not as if he is trying to work out his own place in that chaotic circus. 'I don't fit into it! I never have! It's just the way I am. I never had any desire to fit into it and maybe that is because of where I grew up. I never had a plan to make a living out of it. I was just doing what I like doing.'

And somehow he has found a way to make a life out of it, for now. Cornwall will always be his home, but after that day at Aileen's and the permanent association of Riley's with the spirit of his sister Cherry and with the great times he has had there, Clare has begun to seep into his soul. 'Cornwall's part of me. I love it. My family's there, my nephews are there. So yeah. But I always had a good feeling here. The land and the sea feel the same. But there is more space here than in Cornwall. Loads more space. I am just drawn to here. I feel more comfortable here. The place feels right to me.'

When their baby was born in Galway in the New Year, he and Riv called her Eiva because it means 'little bird'. 'When she first started moving, we were saying that she fluttered like a little bird.' Mickey thinks for a while when asked if becoming a father has changed anything about the pursuit that began when he was an eight-year-old boy in Cornwall happily abandoning himself to the white surf. 'Not really. I am more appreciative of what we have got here, that it is so special. It makes me . . . Before I would get a bit stirred up about things. Now it just makes me laugh.'

9

Day Is Done

In 2012, summer waltzed in early. The last Monday of March
was perfect. The schools were off for Easter holidays and just
like that the seaside towns of the west, stunned by the sun-
burst, fell into high-season rhythms. In the cafés and bars the
radios were crackling with two news items. Bertie Ahern, the
longest-serving Taoiseach in the history of the state, handed
in his resignation from Fianna Fáil, the party he had led for
over a decade, before the expected motion to expel him was
put forward. It was the last act of the man who had guided
Ireland through the fast years. The other talking point was
the eternal Irish talking point: the weather. It was nineteen
degrees Celsius and balmy – in March! It was further proof
that the weather systems were all messed up.

But on this day, nobody in Clare was too worried about that.
In the heat and under flawless blue skies, the prime colours of
the fields and the sea and the bare stone of the Burren took on

a super-saturated quality. Foreign visitors wandering across those fields and taking photographs seemed dazed by it all, as if they had stepped into a John Hinde postcard. Suddenly the winding roads were filled with roadsters and convertibles. The seaside town of Lahinch swooned as if it was the height of some vintage July day. The promenade was crowded with strollers wearing shorts and shades and the early signs of sunburns. The dogs looked parched. The ice-cream vendors had eagerly set up stall. The tide was busy with skinny kids in wetsuits getting surf lessons. Tee-off times on the golf course were at a premium. And, as always happens in Ireland during rare bursts of beautiful weather, everything slowed down a little bit and became a little bit dreamy. People smiled and remarked that it would be some country if it could be like this all the time.

But the real gift was that the weather arrived with a swell which produced a full week of waves that varied between commanding and brilliant. The sunshine was so true that even the crashing waters underneath Moher looked inviting.

Just like that, Clare became a dreamscape.

Tom Doidge-Harrison had arrived early in the morning. He had just got home from two months in Spain with his family and expected to be greeted by the usual gales and wicked spirits of March. But the cliffs were as tranquil as he had ever known them, and below them Aileen's was breaking steadily.

He was standing on the headland watching the wave when the familiar figure of John McCarthy came gambolling across the field, his face lit up in a big smile. They hadn't seen each other for many months. Indeed McCarthy was half surprised to find himself there: as he had predicted, surfing had taken a back seat since he and Rachel had had their baby girl, Rebecca. But the morning was irresistibly beautiful and he found himself doing what he hadn't done for an age: grabbing his board and taking off. They stood at the edge of the cliff together and felt the familiar tingle that watching Aileen's brings about.

'I don't think that wave has become any less of a novelty because you can never master it,' Doidge-Harrison said later that day, standing in the area on top of the cliff where the cars are parked. He was in cracking form but, as ever, he was racing on, eager to spend some time at home and to plane some boards that evening. 'It was just a lovely feeling heading out there with John today. We had the whole place to ourselves and just had that feeling of . . . Well, it's like being kids. And it's a great way to catch up with someone you like. Just a brilliant social thing to do.'

In the months after Rebecca was born, surfing had come to feel an even smaller part of McCarthy's life. But walking down the goats' trail with Doidge-Harrison, yapping about father-hood and glorying in the relative quietness of the place – he confessed he was amazed that there was nobody else around that morning – brought everything about the previous two decades of his life rushing back. 'We stood at the bottom of the rock ready to paddle out and I had not been out there for quite a long time. I am at that point where I can forget about surfing. But just then I remembered that I really do love this and it is such an important part of my life. Sometimes I think of it as small. But that day with Tom brought it home, and it was magical and special.'

In the six years since McCarthy and Doidge-Harrison first

surfed at Aileen's, both of their lives had changed immeasurably. The time was when they would have been surprised not to meet each other on a morning like this. Now, they savoured every second. For all they knew this would be the last time they ever had Aileen's all to themselves.

By mid-afternoon the place was busy. Dan Skajarowski came running across the field at one point, waving as he passed. At the top of the cliffs Trish Blount was watching Dave out surfing. Their baby girl, Ellody, was fanned out on a rug, shaded from the sun. She would sleep through the drama unfolding far below. The Blounts live just minutes from the headland, but by the time they arrived McCarthy had left. Dave and John are as tight now as when they were children but scheduling their lives so they can surf together is no longer as easy. Dave's energy for surfing remained undiluted after Ellody's birth, though the everyday dangers involved do cross his mind from time to time. But he keeps them in perspective. 'I know that just driving from the house to Ennis is as dangerous. Who knows, a few bad hammerings could change my mind about the type of waves I want to surf. And the days will come when I am going out less and less. But the way I feel now, there are a lot of things I want to do out there still, primarily in paddling.'

Fergal Smith and Tom Lowe were out on the water with Dave and the waves were bold and well sculpted, and they kept on coming. There were a few other people lounging on the warm grass and keeping an eye on the surfing. After a while Tom Gillespie came traipsing down the headland. He had been out in the water all week and was nursing a bit of a cold, but he was grinning from ear to ear because he was flying to Tahiti in early April and then on to Australia for a few months. He was, as always, in brilliantly cheerful form.

Seamus McGoldrick had hoped to travel with Gillespie but, as ever, Seamus had about five different projects on the go at once. The Sligo man's winter had gone by in a blur: he'd worked on a shellfish farm and in a restaurant to keep body and soul together and spent all his free time putting together an Irish team for the inaugural World Bodyboarding Championships in the Canary Islands. Then, in early spring, he'd made some short bodyboarding films with a friend before taking off for France, and when he returned he didn't have the money to go travelling with Gillespie. So he sent him an email wishing him all the best. 'I was happy for him and dead jealous too. But he was flying out to Tahiti on a Friday and there was a ten-foot swell forecast for the Monday. So I went from being envious of him to being a bit scared for him.'

A few weeks later, news reached McGoldrick which embellished Gillespie's reputation for being as lucky as a black cat. He had spent a week at Teehupoo, the first Irish bodyboarder to surf the wave, and everything had gone well. Then, towards the end of the week, when he had begun to get to know the wave, he lost his bearings and couldn't see properly because of the mist created by the curl of the wave. He tried cutting through the curtain of water and penetrating the back of the wave but it was too heavy and it just absorbed him. The wave flung him on to the jagged coral reef. He stood up in waist-deep water, only to be confronted with another ten-foot wave crashing in front of him. That one dragged him across the coral bed and then sucked him back into the channel. A group of surfers from Argentina pulled Gillespie into their boat.

He felt his leg pulsing and pulled his wetsuit up to reveal a deep gash filled with dark blood. Not for the first time, Tom found himself in hospital. Not for the first time, he listened to a doctor telling him how lucky he had been: the coral dagger had missed a main artery by millimetres. His maiden visit to Teehupoo had left him with nothing worse than a scar to add to the collection. But he had been fortunate.

'That's Tom,' Seamus says. 'Last I heard from him he was staying in some bodyboarder's house in western Oz. Living the life.'

Ollie O'Flaherty, who had hurled himself into the teeth of a ferocious wave in Mullaghmore just a few weeks earlier, came over to say hello to Trish Blount. The Clare man didn't know it yet but the stars were about to align for him with that nomination (along with Andrew Cotton) in the Wave of the Year category at the ritzy XXL Big Wave Awards in Los Angeles. The ceremony was held in early May and placed the young Clare man among his heroes for the evening. If it was faintly surreal for him, it was also an acknowledgement of the fact that waves breaking off the Irish coast ranked among the most spectacular on the planet. In a strange loop of fate, that day of surfing in Tahiti the previous August, which had tortured Fergal Smith as he stood at the Reading festival, was the story of that awards ceremony. Nathan Fletcher walked away with the Ride of the Year and the Wave of the Year. It was like Smith had said: one day can change everything.

Down below, the waves kept crashing. We followed the figure of Tom Lowe. If anyone has history with Aileen's, it is Lowe. Two years earlier he'd suffered his worst surfing injury under the cliffs when Fergal towed him into a wave which turned out to be pure deception and just crumbled all around him, forcing him to straighten his board and try and bolt from danger. It was no use: the wave fell in on him and ripped his shoulder ligaments – the beginning of a horrible two years. The following summer he was in Tahiti and the same arm got caught inside a wave and was dragged at a weird angle, and the wave rolled him as a wrestler might, forcing him over with the lip while the force of the water mangled the ligaments of his arm all over again. When he arrived home in England he had an operation and was instructed not to surf for eight months. But now, the fact that he could trace the original trouble back to Aileen's wasn't going to stop him from surfing there.

This was the fifth day in a row that Lowe and Smith had been on the water. Surfing can make you greedy about time. They were loath to miss a single minute in the water that week, rising at five every morning so they could stretch and be on their boards first thing. Their day had started at Riley's, and their plan was to return there around tea-time once they had finished at Aileen's. So now Lowe was paddling hard into a promising-looking wave – a decision that would mark the beginning of a long, tough day.

When he began to describe his first mishap of the day he immediately became distracted by the memory of a wave Fergal had surfed as soon as they paddled out. 'We were only just in the water and Fergal did his usual thing of going super-technical on this wave that was – well, I'd call it ten foot solid, Ferg would put it at six to eight foot maximum. It might have been twelve foot. So he got this great wave and you just think: he has done it again. But I was happy for him. And I have changed my tactic out at Aileen's a bit. I sit on the inside ledge and try and get the thicker waves. So I waited out the back for a good thirty and forty minutes. It wasn't cold, it was glassy and dreamy and sunny. And Dave Blount was there – he was waiting for a wave to get out right on the inside, so he was miles away from me. I was right out the back of the wave. And I knew there was a big set coming in because when it is glassy like that you can see big black lumps out on the horizon. But I didn't get too excited because the likelihood of getting a wave when Aileen's is that size and not even breaking on the boil is so small. Then it came in and it was about ten foot and it gave me enough of a let-in to attempt it, so I dug in deep and was scratching into the thing. A wave like that can look steeper and fun from the top angle but it is actually big and quite dangerous. Until you get into the water, you can't really feel the power. Because it felt like a juggernaut had hit me.'

From the cliff top, it seemed as if the tip of Lowe's board had caught in the water and he went from gliding along and holding a perfect line to affecting manic aerobics moves. Then he was coin-flipped in the air and disappeared. What had happened was that once he took off, he grabbed the rail of his board as soon as he realized how hollow the wave was shaping up. And then he understood that this was a different wave to anything he had experienced before.

'I have never paddled into a wave of that size and thickness in Aileen's. Usually the waves are half the size and on the inside ledge. This was from the outside. I knew the thing was a beast. Because at Aileen's you can see when the wave crumbles on that boil – by the "boil" I mean the big boulders that are underneath and are shallow enough to let the wave crumble, and you roll into that. It is like going down a mini-ramp, and then you go down to a steep bowl and you come around and you have this beautiful bowl-shaped wave that is impossible to paddle into, but somehow because of that roll-in you trickle into it. And that is how 99 per cent of the good waves you get there go. But the shape of this wave was a slab – a really hollow wave on take-off with no roll-in and no easy way to get into it. It is just an air-drop down into it. So I grabbed hold of my rail and I disconnected with the wave in the air. When I landed my face was almost on the top of the board. I pulled up on the rail and came around, and by then the wave was over me: I was inside the barrel. I just saw this big green beautiful thing going over me and everything was slowing down. The whole thing probably took four seconds. I was right in it where I was supposed to be. But I had no balance: I ended up with two hands on the nose of my board, my back foot off the surfboard and my front foot still on, and my two hands on the nose. That is unheard of unless you are some kind of barrel master like Jamie O'Brien or John John Florence. But maybe not at Aileen's, I dunno. So I went to put my foot back down and it was the water, not the board, and that is how I fell off.'

In surfing, these leaps into genuine danger happen so fast that they can go unnoticed. Halfway down the cliffs, Kevin Smith was just beginning to pack his camera up when he saw Lowe transform into a whirling dervish before him. Smith fell into his lifeguard's habits: he began counting and scanning the water as the wave spread and lost its energy. He counted ten and then twenty seconds without seeing Lowe surface.

During those moments Lowe spent scrabbling around under the water, he knew he was utterly on his own. The wave kept surging towards the ocean floor and carried him as a passenger. He felt his ears wanting to pop, as if he was in an aeroplane approaching the runway, and could feel the pressure of the water beginning to tighten around his body. If he opened his eyes, he knew the water would be black. And he was spinning like a weathervane in a storm. His limbs were thrashing in all directions. It was anyone's guess as to which way the surface was. 'You just kind of relax, if you can. Just telling yourself to relax gives you maybe five seconds of just being chilled and waiting for it to pass. I've learned not to panic like that. But then I felt myself coming up after ten seconds and was beginning to think: wow, that was hardcore but I am through it, I am up. And the motion is like a whirlpool, and it can spit you out or back in there. And I felt myself going down again for another ten seconds.'

Twenty seconds turned into thirty. When Lowe is in the barrel of the wave he has his mouth wide open, so he'd had no time to take a gulp of air before going under. One second he was surfing, the next he had no air in his lungs and was trying not to drown.

'The whole thing was not controlled. I knew if I went straight after that drop I was getting a lip on the head. I don't want to mess about picking the wrong lines or going straight. I was gasping for water and gagging. So I was taking in sea water and I remember having a few mouthfuls and you can feel it going in yet you know the lungs are gasping for something. Still, I knew I wasn't drowning . . . Fergal didn't pull me up half-unconscious so I'm not going to make a drama out of it. But if I'm being honest, it shook the shit out of me that this could happen on such a calm glassy day with big lulls. I really wanted that wave and it gave me exactly what I wanted.

I wanted a really heavy tow-style wave and I reckoned I could make it at the back end. Because on the forehand I don't rate myself as very good at taking off late. I am not as technical as Fergal. But on my back side I feel more confident taking off underneath waves. I just prefer backhand barrel riding. I don't think I'm that good at weaving through barrels and making ten-second barrels. I am just a bit of a unit at holding my rail. And Aileen's said: here you go. Then it taught me a lesson.'

He was still dazzled by the sunlight when he heard the drone of the jet-ski announcing Smith's arrival. Within seconds Fergal had hauled him on to the back of the ski and was aiming for the pier in Doolin. Lowe's surfboard was gone. He was hunched over on the ski coughing up salt water and spent the journey trying to get some air into his lungs. By the time they reached the pier, though, he had applied the usual reasoning to what had happened. He had been fine! He had gotten away with it! And he knew he didn't want to quit for the day. So at Doolin they hauled the jet-ski out of the water, fixed the trailer to the van, changed quickly and headed straight to Riley's, snacking on biscuits and fruit. 'Whatever we could lay our hands on at that moment. We were just thinking about getting to the next place.'

It was around tea-time when they were back in the water. Riley's was quiet: most people had had their fill of waves by this stage. They figured they might have an hour of surfing. Ollie O'Flaherty was there and a New Zealander named Ollie Adams was in the water. They took turns towing in on the ski. Again, Fergal struck gold almost as soon as they were in the water. Not for the first time, Lowe found himself lost in admiration for his friend. 'He just had two beauties – probably the best waves he ever got out there. Just seeing that gives you a great feeling. Fergal's always been far beyond his years in ability and skill but he has this maturity. When it comes to heavy waves, only the really good guys who are out there understand him. It's never been about trying to prove himself or getting the biggest wave or the wipe-out of the day for him. Sometimes he will sit there not ripping or charging at all. Then he does something like that. It is because he is there for the long haul so he will put the time in, and in the long term he will get the best waves, because of that reason.'

At around seven o'clock the sun began to fade and they were thinking of calling it a day. But the weather was so mellow and golden that even the desolate rock shelf at Riley's looked pretty. Lowe decided he would have just one last wave. They were all tired and fairly battered but really contented after five full days of big combative waves. He lined a wave up and Fergal towed him in.

A week later, sitting on the couch in Mickey Smith's house with his leg in a cast, Tom Lowe laughed ruefully and said, 'There was pure goodness in that wave.'

Kevin Smith was on the headland filming and caught the next few seconds at a perfect angle. When Lowe studied the frames he could content himself that he had done nothing wrong. 'I let go of the rope early, so I was right where I wanted to be, behind the horseshoe, back-dooring the wave. When you look back at video you often criticize yourself but I wouldn't have placed myself anywhere else. But when I was looking at the footage there was just one little kink. There is a corner in that reef that produces a perfect horseshoe-shaped bowl. It's like a semi-circle. But there is also a sudden drop, a step in front of the entrance to the wave, so if you don't get down the wave in time you either have to olly down – and no one does that, we don't wear straps – or bottom turn around it or time it right so you are over it before it forms and then you are in the barrel. So I went over the initial corner of the reef and I was coming out and there was just this other little bump in there, enough to affect your momentum and line. You can see in the film that the outside rail got this little touch and then it was this mad misty flip inside this barrel; I cartwheeled backwards, then went up with the barrel, and then I connected.'

Or rather, he slammed into the unforgiving rock surface that lies beneath the water.

'It felt like running and kicking a brick wall as hard as I could.'

He surfaced just in time for another wave to hit him and wash him into a hollow where waves are always crashing and ebbing, creating a constant current. He ducked under the next wave, half swam, half floated through the surf and gave a thumbs-up sign to Fergal Smith. From the headland it looked as if he was fine. But he got on to the back of the jet-ski gingerly and this time he was completely doubled over. A numbing pain was beginning to shoot through his foot and his head was pounding. The toll of the last five days had robbed him of the last of his adrenalin.

'I'd never imagined that breaking something could be so painful. I'd broken my wrist and arm before but they were just little aches. That was . . . Poor Fergal, I was more or less hugging him on the way back to the pier. I clung on like a limpet – I was giving him a good old-fashioned hug. I just needed that contact. I was almost lying down and my leg was resting on the ski and Fergal was trying not to hit any bumps. Which was more or less impossible.'

It was nearly eight o'clock and beginning to get dark by the time they pulled into the pier at Doonbeg. The place was deserted. Tom sat against the wall of the pier not far from the water's edge. Banged-up fishing boats and nets were all about him. He was wearing a jacket over his wetsuit and Fergal had given him a flask with something hot in it. He was pale under his tan but still tried to raise a grin about the predicament and admitted that he looked a sorry sight. Fergal had slipped into a combination of logistics supremo and brisk matron, making phone calls and figuring out the fastest way to get his friend to hospital, hauling the jet-ski up the ramp, whipping off his wetsuit and climbing into jeans and a jumper, all the time chatting away.

On the way over to Ennis, Mickey Smith, who was working in England, happened to phone to see how the day had gone. Tom told him of his mishap, poking fun at himself. You could tell he was pleased to hear from his friend. Because Lowe lives in Spain he is acutely aware of the dynamic between the three of them. He sometimes feels a little guilty about the idea of appearing whenever the waves are good. 'Fergal is the guy who maintains the ski, checks the safety and keeps the engine running whereas I am abroad in the sunshine. Before we started tow-in surfing together, we were just great mates. We were very different people with different upbringings but we clicked. Then you go buy jet-skis and equipment together and it gets more complicated: you have to be strong friends not to have arguments. We don't, but there is that tension because it is our life. We have different styles. Mickey stays out of it a lot.

He is just this creative guy who calls the shots and then creates this magic. But since Mick and Riv had Eiva, Fergal's been the one calling the shots as to where we should go and what we should be filming. And that is fine: his judgement is excellent. So when we are together, Fergal does his patient, calculating thing and I do mine. I dunno . . . People think that I feel I have to prove myself or that I want to push myself to the point of killing myself. It is not that. It is just the enjoyment of pushing myself as hard as I can.'

Tess was waiting at the petrol station at nine o'clock. Customers filling their tanks at the time could not have failed to notice the peculiar sight of a man in a wetsuit and snowboarding gear hopping across the courtyard into the back of a van. There was a bench/bed waiting for him. They knew from experience that the smartest thing was to go straight to the hospital in Limerick. After a sunny Monday they were optimistic that the casualty department would be reasonably quiet.

Lowe knew what he looked like when he wandered in the door at ten that night: sun-kissed and blond and generally like an advertisement for the outdoors life – the enviable life. He knew he wasn't going to be high priority, regardless of the pain. Still, the eight-hour wait the receptionist told him to expect seemed excessive. They found themselves sitting in the van and contacted some friends, who offered to put Tom up for the night so he could return to the hospital in the morning. 'I didn't know these people at all so it was nice of them. Wasn't my best moment either – showing up at someone's house in a stinking wetsuit. Wasn't in the best of states. Crawled into the shower in this person's house and then lay awake all night.

When I got back to the hospital in the morning I was told I had missed my place in the queue. So I sat there and it was two o'clock in the afternoon when I was seen.'

The thing is, Lowe finds it impossible not to keep his good side out. He hadn't eaten anything except an arnica tablet since the previous afternoon and the pain was tortuous. But he smiled at the hospital staff and assured them that he had nothing better to do anyway. He is helplessly polite and laid back, and this seemed to amuse the staff. 'To be honest,' he laughs, 'I probably sounded like a bit of a . . . not a cheese-ball but, you know, a surf dude. And they gave me a good ripping. I like the Irish staff. They are putting their hours in and working their arses off. I am not giving out to them for not seeing me sooner, that's for sure. There are people in there with God knows what wrong with them and there is bugger all staff so I was happy to wait my turn. So I was pretty mellow and they were having fun with that. "Oohhh, bit of a free spirit, are ya? Got a bit too big for your boots?" Giving me a bit of shit. It was fun. But yeah, they want to know what the hell we are doing surfing above rocks. It's a point, I suppose.'

Lowe spent the next week with his leg propped up on pillows in Mickey Smith's house. Yanni came over from Spain. The sublime weather continued and Fergal kept on surfing from dawn to dusk, never tiring, never stopping. Then the clouds gathered, the wind dropped, and the sea became a lake.

And that was it. April and May were wash-outs. June and July were filled with glum, deadened weather. The spark of summer was rarely seen. Day after day of mild weather and gentle swells and baby waves, and often nothing at all. The frustration came with the territory. 'Just nothing,' Bill Keane sighed. 'Wasn't a great winter. That's the way it goes. I'm starting to think I need to get away to the sunshine.'

Fergal Smith is fortunate in that his patience extends to dry land. When there are no waves he uses his time to get the rest of his life in order, working on the vegetable patch he had been thinking about all winter and servicing the skis and sitting down with Kevin and Mickey to select the best pieces of film they shot that year. His year's work was going to be distilled into this small package of film which he would forward to Adam Warren at Analog so it could be worked into a full-length documentary about the surfers under the company's sponsorship. They had suggested to Smith that he come out to Hawaii in the winter so he could feature along with some of the others. But he persuaded them that those shots wouldn't be a true representation of who he was as a surfer, that brackish Irish skies and jagged cliffs are the backdrop to his waves.

Mickey combed through the hours of footage they had taken and refined them into a montage of Fergal gliding through the huge ocean glaciers. It was a full year of his life – all the dawn alarm clocks and the drudgery of launching the jet-ski and throwing himself into the Atlantic even though his lips were blue with cold and then spending four or five hours alone in the water, infinitely patient and watchful, just to see if he could surf the next wave better than he had surfed the thousands before. And sometimes the next wave didn't even come along. The film was his book of evidence, a further vindication for living his life on his terms. It is powerful and hauntingly beautiful, and it is short. It hammers home the basic truth that even the most accomplished surfers have to accept: even when they fall into synchronicity with the most perfect wave, it can only last a few seconds.

When the film was done, he felt he could take it easy. He wanted to use the long break to give his body some rest. Fergal Smith has been chasing waves relentlessly since he jumped on a train in Westport on the afternoon he completed his Leaving Certificate. He vowed that he was going to spend a full summer in Ireland, regardless of how tame the surf was.

'He kept telling me that,' Bill Keane says. 'Have to say, I couldn't see it working out.'

In May, Fergal and Kevin were at home surfing an empty beach one day when Kevin came off his board awkwardly and thumped his back. The pain was jarring but he presumed it was no different to the hundreds of tumbles he had taken and he told Fergal to keep surfing. But Kevin struggled to get his breath for a few days and when he went for an X-ray they told him he had broken his back. Six weeks of lying in a neck brace and doing nothing was prescribed.

In July, Fergal went on a week-long retreat, switching the phone off and just tuning out for a few days. When he checked his laptop, all the surf and weather sites were highlighting a thrilling break in Fiji. Immediately his mind was racing: two days left . . . could he get a flight? . . . when would he arrive? But he convinced himself to skip it, to stay put. On the phone he sounded fairly proud of his self-discipline. There would be other swells. He would stay firm this summer!

The next evening he phoned, sounding a little sheepish and a lot excited. 'Going to Tahiti in the morning. Not sure when I'll be back.'

Whenever Fergal Smith leaves Clare for his periodic jaunts,

the ineffable energy he brings to the local surfing spot vanishes with him. When he left for Tahiti Mickey Smith was still on a filming job in England, so for the first time in a while they were both out of Clare. When they are gone, Aileen's or Riley's or Bumbaloids can feel bigger and lonelier. But the thing about this group is that it can and eventually will disperse just as naturally as it came together. There was never a grand plan. The water brought them here and it is keeping them here.

But for how long? One evening in April Dave Blount sat in his living room and thought for a moment about how long this accidental gathering would go on for. It was one of those nuisance evenings of spitting drizzle and ever-darkening skies, the latest in a series of days that made them realize just how much surfing Irish waters made them work for their deserts. Nobody had caught a decent wave in weeks. 'People come and go,' Blount remarked. 'If Mickey and Fergal left there would be a blip in terms of what is going on here. The two of them are a huge part of the explosion that has happened here in Clare. Myself and Trish talk now about when Ellody gets to school age that it would be nice to live somewhere where she could walk to school. We may go eventually, but it is perfect here now. And I think the number of people surfing the good waves around here is going to keep growing. In a way I feel sorry for the young kids now because they have all these waves here on their doorstep and they think this is what they have to measure up to even though it is one of the heaviest waves on planet Earth. It is in at the deep end for them. They feel they have to go tow in at Riley's on a fifteen-foot day. That brings its own challenges and problems.

'I would rather not see the crew here disperse. I do feel as if they are here long term. I think Fergal is here long term. I think Mickey and Riv like it here. I know I need more of a security blanket than Mickey does. You know, Mick is like a teenager who never grew up. And I mean that as a compliment. He is a guy who had these ideals and ways of doing things as a teenager and they are fully intact today. He never compromised. He loves what he does. And there are elements that grate on him. Still, compared to office work or digging ditches, it is a dream.'

And that's exactly what this whole thing is: something that exists right on the border of reality and make-believe. They might leave Lahinch and not meet again but there can be no end to it – whatever 'it' even is. Surfing is a succubus, and it offers them no promises or guarantees. None of them can be sure what is going to happen next winter or the winter after that or where they will be in ten winters' time. Fergal Smith might be the best at his game in Ireland but very few people know who he is. And he likes it that way just fine.

Surfing, though, is becoming more popular by the season. A few years ago John McCarthy thought it would always be considered a luxury pursuit. 'But then I understood that in the summer, with the weather here, it is the opposite. It is one of the few ways we can get kids out in the fresh air when it is raining.' And heads are turning. There is a small but growing band of youngsters out there whose imaginations have been sparked not by the ultra-bright allure of Premiership football or the localized glory awaiting them on Gaelic fields but by the idea of being what Fergal Smith is: a lone panther moving with impossible lightness. But surfing promises nothing more than fleeting thrills. When Smith has a spare moment, he thinks about what he wants to do with whatever influence he has, using his website to promote ideas like conservation and respecting the environment. And somehow to communicate the fact that for all its rewards, this life is not for everyone.

There is absolutely no security in what any of them do. And there is a contradiction at the heart of surfing: for all the limitless freedom it gives them, it exacts its own terms. It has defined the way they live their lives. They are restless people, and they gladly forsake the material stuff and the conventional ambitions just so they can take advantage of the wildest days on the west of Ireland, when the world is cowering indoors and they feel like they have inherited all the riches of the land.

'It is about finding a balance,' Steph Skajarowski said quietly one day. 'It is simpler for someone like Fergal who can do it as a career. And he deserves it because what he does is incredible. And if Fergal was in any other sport in the world he would probably be making a lot more money. But that is surfing in Europe, let alone Ireland. There are guys like Shambles and Dan who are very good but probably won't make money out of this at all. Seamus is a bright boy and that is where the decision needs to be made for him. The thing is, if this all dried up tomorrow, if the banks shut down and the economy went completely wallop, I don't think any of their lives would change a great deal. They would all find a way. Even if they had to walk to the beach with their surfboards under their arms, they would do it. When you are growing up you don't have money. I work part time during the winters and in January and February I just have to watch the pennies a bit more. So money, that whole thing, it doesn't change the way their lives go on a day-to-day basis.'

The day is the whole show. On that last Monday in March, the Cliffs of Moher Experience was crowded with day-trippers and coach tours. When you pay the nominal fee to walk up the circular stairs to the viewing deck of O'Brien's tower, you get a complimentary brochure. It bears the usual images on the front – birdlife, the tower itself and panoramic shots of the cliffs. But there is also a photograph of a lone surfer flaming through a wave, a magnificent wave, a black wall of Atlantic water giving way to snow-white surf, its tip lit by the sun. None of the surfers had ever seen the brochure and they were amused to learn that they had been incorporated into the tourist experience. (In fact, Fáilte Ireland had once given Fergal some sponsorship money but they didn't renew the relationship last year. He had no hard feelings: he thought the lady he was dealing with was completely sound but they decided to allocate the budget elsewhere. It wasn't as if they were going to make or break him one way or the other anyway: of the multi-million-euro budget Fáilte Ireland has to promote the country, they had been giving Fergal a thousand euros per annum. You think of all the people who have seen the photographs and film of Smith humanizing that wave and those cliffs and you can't help but think that they are missing a trick.)

It's a funny thing. The Cliffs of Moher have this supernatural draw on visitors: it is where they all come when they visit Ireland. But few people stand on the precipice for very long. Even on a sublime day it is an unsettling place. Samaritan signs are posted subtly but strategically on wooden posts near the very edge of the headland. Those cliffs and the vast Atlantic and that sheer fall make visitors feel as if they are standing on the very edge of civilization. People take a deep breath when they step up to the platform and look out past Carraig Na Trail. Sometimes you can hear them inhale sharply because the starkness and scale of the view are shocking. There isn't much conversation there.

It is a place that holds an obvious attraction for photography enthusiasts, and a lot of people up there that Monday were packing serious-looking equipment. Some people noticed the surfers straight away, pointing at them as they sat on their boards in a loose semi-circle in the water. In mid-afternoon, shortly before Tom Lowe went under, the cliff face across from O'Brien's tower was busy with tiny surfers climbing down the goats' trail and clambering across the big smooth stones at the very base of Moher. From this height they looked like Allingham's Little Men brought to life.

And just by being there they make the Cliffs of Moher seem a little less remote but no less magical. What they are doing down there is no different from what Michel Petit, that crazy, beautiful Frenchman, did back on a muggy August morning in 1974 when he strung a wire between the two monstrous towers of the World Trade Center and walked between them. By paddling out from the shadow of the cliffs and attempting to gather in their little coven around the wave, they help us to understand the scale and majesty of what we are looking at.

Near the path on the way back down to the café and gift shop there is a broad stone platform where Cornelius O'Brien created a circular stone picnic table. If you look closely you can see the metal rivets that fastened the table into the stone; storms did away with the table itself decades ago. But one of the information boards on the path carries a photograph that tells you all you need to know about the Cliffs of Moher. It must be around a hundred years old, and in it you can see a shadowy figure sitting at the table in front of two bottles. Two other people are standing at the edge of the platform and what looks like a child is sitting down. The platform and cliff face have been brightened by the sun: it seems like a nice day. The people all look as if they are caught in the moment, lost in their private worlds, allowing the majesty of the place to grab their souls for a few minutes. What would they make of their cliffs if they could see them on this day? And what would they make of the wonderful madness occurring on the thunderous wave crashing far below?

'There is this classic thing about surfers as they grow up,' John McCarthy said one day. 'The adult surfer says, "Oh yeah, I got the wave and I rode it the whole way to the beach!" But when you talk to a five-year-old who has just surfed, he or she will say, "Oh, the wave picked me up and brought me the whole way to the beach." Instead of the focus being I-did-this-on-the-wave, it is the-wave-did-this-to-me. And I think over time the focus will be on Aileen's. On the cliff. On the beauty of it. And for me, all of this is about the creator of it all rather than the individuals. And the glory will go elsewhere over time. And young guys are going to rise up. There will be a new Fergal Smith – even though I think Fergal is going to be around for a long, long time and I do think he has brilliant days ahead of him. And someone who has seen Mickey's photographs and who was inspired by those will come along wanting to take their own images. The day will come when there are new people there and it will be their moment. But the wave will always be there.'

Perhaps that is why Fergal Smith and Tom Lowe and the others have thrown themselves into this life so completely. From the beginning, they have been on borrowed time.

So if you are ever up at the cliffs and you see them down there, do not forget to salute them. Yes, see them and salute their boldness, and remember that this strange, eccentric passion is their life. Remember too that of the thousands of people who have been drawn to the cliffs, you are seeing something that Cornelius O'Brien or John Huston did not see when they stood on the headland looking out at the endless Atlantic.

So try and see them moving through one of those great eternal waves if you can, and remember that they are, like all of us, just passing through.

Picture Acknowledgements

Page 1. Photo of Fergal Smith © Mickey Smith.

Page 2. Photo of Fergal Smith © Mickey Smith.

Page 3. Portrait photos of (left) Fergal Smith and (right) Mickey Smith, and the photo of Mickey Smith on the cliffs © Rivie.

Page 4. Photos of Mickey Smith with his sister Cherry at the Reading Festival, and (left) Cherry's son Riley are courtesy of Mickey Smith. Portrait photo of John McCarthy © Rivie.

Page 5. Photo of Dan Skajarowski © Mickey Smith.

Page 6. Photo of Steph Skajarowski © Mickey Smith. Portraits of Tom Doidge-Harrison with his daughter Nora, Dave Blount and Tom Lowe © Rivie.

Page 7. Photo of Hugo Galloway © Mickey Smith.

Page 8. Photo of Tom Gillespie © Mickey Smith.

Keith Duggan is an award-winning senior sportswriter with *The Irish Times*, for whom he writes features and a weekly column on sports, 'The Sideline Cut'. He is originally from Ballyshannon in County Donegal and lives in Galway.